MW01067826

KEYS TO OPEN HEAVEN

And I also say to you that you are Peter, and on this rock I will build My church, and the gates of Hades shall not prevail against it. And I will give you the keys of the kingdom of heaven, and whatever you bind on earth will be bound in heaven, and whatever you loose on earth will be loosed in heaven (Matthew 16:18-19).

JAMES A. DURHAM

Copyright © 2014 by James A. Durham

Keys to Open Heaven
by James A. Durham

Printed in the United States of America

ISBN 9781498417587

All rights reserved solely by the author. The author guarantees all contents are original and do not infringe upon the legal rights of any other person or work. No part of this book may be reproduced in any form without the permission of the author. The views expressed in this book are not necessarily those of the publisher.

Scripture.quotations taken from the New King James Version (NKJV). Copyright © 1982 by Thomas Nelson, Inc. Used by permission. All rights reserved.

Scripture.quotations taken from the New International Version (NIV). Copyright © 1973, 1978, 1984, 2011 by Biblica, Inc.™. Used by permission. All rights reserved.

Scripture.quotations taken from the King James Version (KJV) – public domain

Scripture.quotations taken from The Message (MSG). Copyright © 1993, 1994, 1995, 1996, 2000, 2001, 2002. Used by permission of NavPress Publishing Group. Used by permission. All rights reserved.

Scripture taken from The One New Man Bible (ONMB), copyright © 2011 William J. Morford. Used by permission of True Potential Publishing, Inc.

Scripture.quotations taken from the Complete Jewish Bible (CJB). Copyright 1998 by David H. Stern, Published by Messianic Jewish Publishers, 6120 Day Long Land, Clarksville, MD 21029, (410) 531d-6644

www.xulonpress.com

TABLE OF CONTENTS

ACKNOWLEDGEMENTS

The entire contents of this book came as gifts from the Lord. Therefore, I want to express my thanks first and foremost to Him for providing the revelation for this book and for the inspiration along the way to complete the project. The Lord is good and His love and mercy endure forever. Without Him none of our works would succeed. It is with gratitude and praise that I acknowledge all He has done to make this book possible.

I want to acknowledge the invaluable assistance I received from my extremely blessed, highly favored, and anointed wife, Gloria. Without her encouragement and assistance this book could never have been completed. For her dedicated and tireless assistance in proof reading the book and confirming the accuracy of the scriptural references I am extremely grateful. I also want to acknowledge my daughter, Michelle, who remains a constant and consistent cheerleader throughout the process of all my writings. Anytime I needed encouragement, I had only to turn to either of these two wonderful ladies. I am so thankful to the Lord that He placed them in my life and constantly blesses me through their love and support!

PREFACE

From an early age, I had a fascination with keys. I started a key collection when I was very young. A key collection was not an easy hobby in those days. People didn't want to give you the keys to their locks. Keys were seldom discarded as long as the locks worked. Yet, I persisted in this hobby as if driven by some inward and unknown force. Over time, my collection grew until I had several large key rings full of old keys. Looking back, I wonder why I wanted to have this collection. The keys didn't really open anything in my small childhood world. Yet, I cherished them. It was several years later that I began to realize that the Lord was working in me at that time to prepare me for something being released now.

When I was growing up in a small town in Oklahoma, people seldom locked their doors. There was a sense of security which was pervasive in our world at that time. When we needed to lock the door as we left town for a few days, we often had difficulty finding the key because it had not been used in a very long time. This was not really a big problem. We could do down to the local department or hardware store and purchase a replacement. There were only a few different designs for door keys during those days. It was likely that the key to my door would also work in your door. A locked door simply said to visitors, "We are not home right now! Please come back when we are here!"

A spirit of trust was a big part of the American culture at that time. Automobiles and trucks also had door keys which were seldom used. No key was necessary to start vehicles since they all had push button ignitions. Today, my van has a push button ignition, but you must have the electronic key with you or it will not start. That was not a problem when I was young. You just got in, pushed the button, put it into gear and drove away. It wasn't necessary to lock things because you simply trusted that no one would use your car or truck without your permission. That was a kinder and gentler time of peace and security. I miss those days. I feel sorry for the young people today who have never experienced this security. One day it will be like that again when we are with the Lord forever in the New Heaven.

In the past few years, I've noticed that I am again experiencing an increasing interest in keys. My collection of keys continues to grow. As I travel to other cities and nations, my eyes are always drawn to the keys which may be on sale in various stores and gift shops. My collection contains keys of all sizes, shapes, and designs. Many key makers are very creative with their designs and their work often looks more like art than functional keys. Some of my favorite keys these days were acquired on one of our many visits to Israel. Recently, the Lord has been speaking to me about keys related to Israel. But, more about that later.

As I prepared to write this book the Lord continued to speak to me about His Kingdom Keys. I began to write down some of my thoughts and turn them into lesson plans for ministry. Then the Lord put it into my heart to write all these down in a book so they could be available to others. As I was writing these things for you and others to read, more revelation kept coming concerning additional Kingdom Keys which the Lord wants to release for us. I hope that you will also begin to collect kingdom keys as you read my experiences with the Lord.

A few years ago, the Lord gave me an amazing vision in which I met Him in Heaven and was given a key ring with five golden keys. Over a period of several weeks the Lord taught me the significance of these Kingdom Keys. I wrote about these keys and the revelation given by the Lord in more detail in the book, "Gatekeepers Arise!" The vision from the Lord which initiated this exploration of Kingdom Keys follows:

A Vision: Tuesday, September 11, 2012

This morning I met Jesus as soon as I arrived in His Heavenly Place. He was standing just inside the entrance and was extending His hand to me with a large gold ring holding several keys. The keys on the ring were also made of gold and the entire thing seemed to be on fire with the glory of the Lord. The Lord asked me if I wanted the keys. I was a little concerned because they seemed to be on fire, and I didn't want to get burned. But, I was convinced that if He wanted me to have them, I should take them. So, I answered the Lord with a simple "Yes!" Then the Lord said, "These are for you! Use them wisely in accordance with the Word!"

I accepted the keys and took them from the Lord's open hand. Please understand that this vision is not just about me. I understood very clearly that these keys are for you as well. Decide now if you want to receive them and use them in obedience to the Lord. After receiving the keys I prayed for wisdom and revelation to understand all that was intended by this gift and the commission which goes with it.

I immediately understood in my spirit by the inspiration of the Holy Spirit that there were five different types of keys on the ring given by the Lord. First, the Holy Spirit led me to Isaiah 22:22, "*I will place on his shoulder the key to the house of David; what he opens no one can shut, and what he shuts no one can open."* This was the key which unlocked Jesus' destiny and identified His purpose. He was to be the one who would sit on the throne of David and rule forever. One of the keys given this morning was to unlock the destiny of each recipient. Receive this Kingdom Key and let the Lord unlock your destiny! Amen?

If you have received prophetic words or revelations from the Lord identifying your destiny, but you have not been able to step into it yet, I believe that you can receive the key which will open it up for you now. Time is short. We don't have time to delay moving toward our destiny. We need to be in it right now. Receive the key! Unlock the door and walk through it!

Next, the Holy Spirit led me to Matthew 16:19, *"And I will give you the keys of the kingdom of heaven, and whatever you bind on earth will be bound in heaven, and whatever you loose on earth will be loosed in heaven."* I understood that there are three types of keys included in this teaching. First, there are the keys to open heaven for others and to bind and loose things in accordance with His Word.

The second key is given to unlock some of the key principles concerning the Kingdom of God. The Lord revealed to me that there are some key kingdom concepts which we have not yet fully learned. Some of the keys offered by the Lord are these principles which will open the door to our understanding. The Lord is going to unlock your understanding in the same way Jesus did this for the disciples on the way to Emmaus. You may not understand it at the moment, but the Lord will suddenly reveal the fullness of these kingdom concepts. Even now, open your spirit and your mind so the Lord can release the Spirit of Wisdom and Revelation to make known His way for you!

The third type of kingdom key is related to what Jesus said in Luke 17:20-21, *"Now when He was asked by the Pharisees when the kingdom of God would come, He answered them and said, "The kingdom of God does not come with observation; nor will they say, 'See here!' or 'See there!' For indeed, the kingdom of God is within you.'"* Jesus is giving each of us the keys to guard our own hearts. Each of us is a gatekeeper over our own heart, home and family. We must be careful what we allow in and what we release to go out.

Gatekeepers are given spiritual discernment to clearly see the difference between the clean and the unclean – between what is holy and what is unholy. We must always guard our own hearts because we are the temple of God. Keys are given by the Lord to bind and loose things within us. These keys are given to close doors to our heart which might let things come in to harm us in spirit, soul, or body. The Lord is also giving us the keys to open our hearts to the Father, the Son and the Holy Spirit so that they may dwell more fully within us. Amen?

The last of the five keys given by the Lord is identified in Revelation 1:18, *"I am He who lives, and was dead, and behold, I am alive forevermore. Amen. And I have the keys of Hades and of Death."* The Lord is giving these keys to us so that we can lock the gates of hell and the grave in the lives of those we lead to the Lord. Every person who fully accepts Jesus, loves Him, and obeys Him will have his/her heart opened in order to be the temple of the indwelling Father, Son and Holy Spirit. One powerful benefit of these keys is to release an anointing for us to open the doors of death and hell and to reach in and draw people out as if from the fire itself. I remembered Jude 1:22-23, *"Be merciful to those who doubt; snatch others from the fire and save them; to others show mercy, mixed with fear—hating even the clothing stained by corrupted flesh."*

I pray that you will receive the awesome gift the Lord is offering today! I pray that you will hear His voice offering you the keys, and that you will reach out by faith and take hold of them. I pray that you will be instructed by the Holy Spirit to always use these powerful keys for the Lord's purpose and in accordance with His Word! May the Lord open up your understanding and release an anointing for you to properly administer the working of these keys! Amen and Amen!

(THE VISION ENDED)

I believe that the Lord planted this fascination with keys in me at a very early age to prepare me to receive what He is now releasing. Most of these things are only now being fully revealed in the depth of hearts and minds so that we can know their meaning. The Lord also filled me with a desire to seek knowledge and to understand more about the Kingdom. I am constantly looking for a deeper meaning in the things the Lord reveals to me. I have learned over the years that keys exist in both the natural world and in the spiritual realm. The most important keys are those which open spiritual doors for us. I am so hungry to know Him better, understand Him more fully, and to be more open to His leadership. So, I continue to collect keys, but now for a different reason.

And I also say to you that you are Peter, and on this rock I will build My church, and the gates of Hades shall not prevail against it. And I will give you the keys of the kingdom of heaven, and whatever you bind on earth will be bound in heaven, and whatever you loose on earth will be loosed in heaven (Matthew 16:18-19).

As I continued to collect keys over the years, I started to notice that many of them were designed with the shape of a cross in the center of the locking mechanism. Many other keys, like the one above, have the Hebrew letter "shin" in their design. This character resembles the letter "W." As you look at the key in the picture below you can quickly see the cross in the design. However, you may not have noticed that the cross is made by putting two "shin" characters together. I found this to be a very interesting design. It spoke to me of the need to receive and understand the use of spiritual keys which were released in both the Old Testament and the New Testament.

Figure 1

In the past few years, the Lord has been speaking to me more and more about the presence of an open heaven. As the Lord continued to speak to me, I began to search the scriptures for references to an open heaven. I was amazed at the wealth of information available in the Bible. I pray that the Lord will inspire you to begin to search out these things for yourself and you ministry. For me the central passage is found in the first chapter of the Gospel of Mark:

At that time Jesus came from Nazareth in Galilee and was baptized by John in the Jordan. As Jesus was coming up out of the water, he saw heaven being torn open and the Spirit descending on him like a dove. And a voice came from heaven: 'You are my Son, whom I love; with you I am well pleased' (Mark 1:9-11, NIV).

Notice that heaven was "*torn open.*" This was no small window or a door which could be opened briefly and then closed again. When Jesus came, Father God ripped an opening in heaven which was never to be closed again. That opening is still available today. When the Lord opens something it stays open. Notice how this concept is related to the key to the house of David. This key is specifically given to Yeshua Ha Messiach and through Him it is passed along to us.

The key of the house of David I will lay on his shoulder; so he shall open, and no one shall shut; and he shall shut, and no one shall open (Isaiah 22:22).

This role was fully and finally assigned to Yeshua ha Messiach when He completed His earthly mission of salvation for the Lord's people. Now, He has the keys which can open doors which no man or evil force can close. He can also close doors which can never be opened again. Many people want to see the doors to their past lives, their failures, and their sins closed once and for all. In the same way, they want to see the doors to their destiny, blessings and favor opened forever. Thank the Lord that He sent Yeshua to accomplish all of these things for you and for me. Read aloud the passage below as you ask Him to open and close doors in your life. Then receive it by faith!

And to the angel of the church in Philadelphia write, 'These things says He who is holy, He who is true, He who has the key of David, He who opens and no one shuts, and shuts and no one opens' (Revelation 3:7).

As I continued to search the scriptures for under-standing of the Open Heaven, the Lord was faithful to guide me to a deeper understanding. As I prayed for wisdom and revelation, the Holy Spirit was faithful to reveal more about these spiritual keys. The Lord con-tinues to provide wisdom to assist us to understand how we are to live faithfully under an open Heaven. He also provides revelation about how we can minister more effectively by serving under this same Open Heaven. At times I also refer to this as ministering under the Glory. In the following chapters, I will share what I have received and hopefully inspire you to search for more Kingdom Keys for your own life and work.

CHAPTER 1

KNOWING YESHUA OPENS HEAVEN

KEY 1: YESHUA

I am convinced that it is critically important for us to know these powerful keys to an Open Heaven. In this season, we need access to the Lord and to all that He is pouring out to us from Heaven. I like to say: "It is all about Jesus!" Now I know that it is, in the end, all about Father God and what He has done for us through Yeshua ha Messiach. However, we must remember that there is only one way to get to the Father. The Father has chosen to do it this way. So, He is in essence saying that for this season it is all about Yeshua. Think about it! Think about what Jesus taught:

> *Jesus said to him, "I am the way, the truth, and the life. No one comes to the Father except through Me. If you had known Me, you would have known My Father also; and from now on you know Him and have seen Him"* (John 14:6-7).

Yeshua is the way! He is the only way! Yeshua is the truth! He is the only truth which really matters in this dark and dying world. He is our hope! He is the only hope for our salvation. He is the light of the world! He is the only light which can guide us on this perilous journey through the darkness of this world. He is literally our all in all! Remember what the Word of God says to us in Ephesians 1:22-23, *"And He put all things under His feet, and gave Him to be head over all things to the church, which is His body, the fullness of Him who fills all in all."* This is the Word of the Lord and it is awesome to us! Amen?

This idea of the centrality of Jesus was a struggle for many of his disciples. They had previously been thoroughly trained in the doctrines of man which were prevalent in that day. It was a huge leap of faith for them to accept and believe that Yeshua was also God. Even those closest to Him had to struggle with this idea. It was only after they saw the things He was doing and heard the Father's decrees about Him that they began to understand. When Jesus proclaimed that He was the only way to the Father, it was a challenge for Philip to accept it. See if you can identify with Philip's spiritual challenge.

Philip said to Him, "Lord, show us the Father, and it is sufficient for us." Jesus said to him, "Have I been with you so long, and yet you have not known Me, Philip? He who has seen Me has seen the Father; so how can you say, 'Show us the Father'? Do you not believe that I am in the Father, and the Father in Me? The words that I speak to you I do not speak on My own authority; but the Father who dwells in Me does the works. Believe Me that I am in the Father and the Father in Me, or else believe Me for the sake of the works themselves" (John 14:8-11).

Jesus was not making this up out of His own mind or his personal will. He was not saying this for His own purposes. Many probably saw it that way. However, all these notions were shattered when He rose from the dead. That got their attention, and they were truly ready to listen, however, they still needed to be set free from the limitations of their old wine skins. Jesus had told them that the Spirit of truth was coming to guide them into all truth; but they couldn't receive it until they witnessed the resurrection. They couldn't handle it until the Spirit of truth was released into them. It came when Jesus breathed on them and released it into their spirits.

So Jesus said to them again, "Peace to you! As the Father has sent Me, I also send you." And when He had said this, He breathed on them, and said to them, "Receive the Holy Spirit. If you forgive the sins of any, they are forgiven them; if you retain the sins of any, they are retained" (John 20:21-23).

I am praying for the Lord to breathe on you right now and release a greater anointing of the Holy Spirit. He can do that, and I believe He will. Have you noticed in the book of Acts that the disciples received more than one outpouring of the Holy Spirit? I am praying for you to receive a fresh new outpouring of the Holy Spirit right now. I am asking the Lord to give you boldness to proclaim the Gospel of the Kingdom and to speak the name of Yeshua to those who do not believe in Him. I am asking the Lord to give everyone who is spiritually running on empty another fill-up of the Holy Spirit. If you are tired in your spirit and your fuel tank is running low, this is the season to get filled again. Don't wait another day! Receive it by faith right now! Pray what the disciples living under great persecution prayed!

Now, Lord, look on their threats, and grant to Your servants that with all boldness they may speak Your word, by stretching out Your hand to heal, and that signs and wonders may be done through the name of Your holy Servant Jesus. And when they had prayed, the place where they were assembled together was shaken; and they were all filled with the Holy Spirit, and they spoke the word of God with boldness (Acts 4:29-31).

The passages which follow this account tell us that after this outpouring, *"great grace"* was upon them all. Could you use some *"great grace"* in your life and ministry? When this *"great grace"* comes upon you, you will reap some powerful benefits just as they did when it came to them. There was none among them who lacked anything. Great grace will break off and cast out the spirit of lack. There was none among them who was sick or infirm. Under the Open Heaven they were all healed. Great grace will release to you the Father's promise of a great outpouring from the floodgates of Heaven.

Great grace will accompany your testimony and lead many to the Lord. Great grace will cause all of these things to work in your ministry. Great grace will open the Heavens over you, your family and your church. Great grace will release healings, miracles, signs and wonders to accompany the preaching of the gospel of the kingdom. It will open the way for hundreds to come to the Lord. The Lord is not trying to withhold His blessings from you! He wants to pour out more than you can contain. He has literally torn the heavens open. He made sure that they will never be closed again. Hallelujah! Thank you Lord!

At that time Jesus came from Nazareth in Galilee and was baptized by John in the Jordan. As Jesus was coming up out of the water, he saw heaven being torn open and the Spirit descending on him like a dove. And a voice came from heaven: "You are my Son, whom I love; with you I am well pleased" (Mark 1:9-11, NIV).

Remember that Yeshua has the keys to the house of David. When he opens a door, no man can close it. Meditate on the promise given in Isaiah 22:22-23, *"The key of the house of David I will lay on his shoulder; so he shall open, and no one shall shut; and he shall shut, and no one shall open. I will fasten him as a peg in a secure place, and he will become a glorious throne to his father's house."* Yeshua not only has the key. He is the Key. He has done amazing things for you and for me by opening the Kingdom of God for us. He continues to do this work for us. He keeps the doors open even as the enemy tries to close them.

Father God was so pleased with Yeshua that he literally tore Heaven open. Why would the Father do this? He tore it open so we could hear His voice and know who Yeshua is. The Open Heaven is all about Yeshua! The Father wants you to know the power and authority He has given to the Son. The scriptures tell us that Yeshua can open the heavens with a prayer. He also wants you to know that you can do the same thing if you can accept it by faith. Remember what He promised in John, Chapter 14:

Most assuredly, I say to you, he who believes in Me, the works that I do he will do also; and greater works than these he will do, because I go to My Father. And whatever you ask in My name, that I will do, that the Father may be glorified in the Son. If you ask anything in My name, I will do it (John 14:12-14).

I want you to be released in the fullness of this promise. Read the promises in these lesson over and over. Read them aloud until they are anchored in your heart. Speak them with your own mouth so that you can feed your heart with their power. Let your faith and trust in the Lord open this up to your spirit so that you truly believe it with all your heart. Now, pray these things over yourself, your family and your church, as you read aloud the passage below!

When all the people were baptized, it came to pass that Jesus also was baptized; and while He prayed, the heaven was opened. And the Holy Spirit descended in bodily form like a dove upon Him, and a voice came from heaven which said, "You are My beloved Son; in You I am well pleased" (Luke 3:21-22).

Did you get it? While He prayed, *"the heaven was opened"* for Him and for us. As you pray in the way Yeshua prayed, you can expect the same results. You can expect the heavens to open for you. Do you believe this? Faith is the key to using these Kingdom Keys. You can expect the Holy Spirit to descend in power and with fire. You can expect to hear the Father speaking. Do you believe this? Many people today spend very little time reading and understanding what Jesus said. We have gone through a period when the church preferred to focus on Paul and study what he said.

It is a good thing to study what Paul taught, but only after we have fully absorbed the teachings of Yeshua. I have actually experienced people telling me that what Paul taught cancels what Jesus said. I don't believe this for a minute. Paul was fully committed to preaching Jesus alone. Paul preached the resurrection of Jesus and taught what the Lord gave him to say. He would never presume to speak against the teachings of Jesus. Once you go against the teachings of Yeshua, what is left? It is all about Yeshua, and I want to call the body of Christ back to true discipleship. True disciples do what Jesus commanded.

> *And Jesus came and spoke to them, saying, "All authority has been given to Me in heaven and on earth. Go therefore and make disciples of all the nations, baptizing them in the name of the Father and of the Son and of the Holy Spirit, teaching them to observe all things that I have commanded you; and lo, I am with you always, even to the end of the age."* Amen (Matthew 28:18-20).

Jesus' command is for us to teach new disciples "*to observe all things that I have commanded.*" How can we do that if we do not know what He commanded? How can we do that unless we spend a great deal of time committing His commands into our hearts? The teachings and commands of Jesus must be firmly anchored in your heart if you are going to be enabled to deal with what the enemy has planned for you. These teachings are our spiritual weapons. Without them, we are totally vulnerable to enemy attacks.

I cannot emphasize this enough! Be students of Yeshua ha Messiach! Know what He taught! Know what He commanded! Read His words over and over. Read them aloud. Remember that Yeshua is the Living Word of God. Make it your first priority in teaching to release these words of life to new believers. Tell them over and over until it is firmly anchored in their spirits and in their souls.

> *For Christ has not entered the holy places made with hands, which are copies of the true, but into*

heaven itself, now to appear in the presence of God for us; not that He should offer Himself often, as the high priest enters the Most Holy Place every year with blood of another--He then would have had to suffer often since the foundation of the world; but now, once at the end of the ages, He has appeared to put away sin by the sacrifice of Himself. And as it is appointed for men to die once, but after this the judgment, so Christ was offered once to bear the sins of many. To those who eagerly wait for Him He will appear a second time, apart from sin, for salvation (Hebrews 9:24-28).

Decree aloud with me: "It is all about Yeshua! I shall not forget that it is all about Yeshua! Amen and Amen!" Fully grasping what the writer of Hebrews says in the passage above is critical to our understanding, and it is the key to operating under an Open Heaven. Jesus did it all. He took care of everything that hinders our ability to come to the Lord. He dealt with the sin problem once and for all. He put His blood on the altar in Heaven. His blood healed the breach in our relationship with the Father.

Remember what the writer cautioned for us in Hebrews 10:34-35, "*for you had compassion on me in my chains, and joyfully accepted the plundering of your goods, knowing that you have a better and an enduring possession for yourselves in heaven. Therefore do not cast away your confidence, which has great reward.*" Don't lose your confidence in the Lord. In this amazing and wonderful season of the Lord, we must hold on to the key which opens the heavens for us. We must not let it go! We must not let Him go.

See that you do not refuse Him who speaks. For if they did not escape who refused Him who spoke on earth, much more shall we not escape if we turn away from Him who speaks from heaven, whose voice then shook the earth; but now He has promised, saying, "Yet once more I shake not only the earth, but also heaven" (Hebrews 12:25-26).

Always remember who He is and what He has done for you! He has not abandoned you. He has not left you without resources and the help you need in this dark hour. He is seated in Heaven with the Father, and He has become your greatest intercessor. He is King of kings and Lord of lords, and yet, He has not lost His commitment to be your savior and your helper. Listen to Him and study all He did and said during His earthly ministry!

He is the key! He is the Key to the Open Heaven. He is seated now where He can keep all that He has promised to you safe until the time of His return. Here is some truly amazing news: *"But God, who is rich in mercy, because of His great love with which He loved us, even when we were dead in trespasses, made us alive together with Christ (by grace you have been saved), and raised us up together, and made us sit together in the heavenly places in Christ Jesus,"* (Ephesians 2:4-6). This passage gives one of the powerful keys to help you live and minister under an Open Heaven. Notice that you have already been seated with Him in heavenly places.

Access has been given through the work of the Holy Spirit (Ephesians 2:18). You cannot be blocked from your inheritance in Heaven. You already have it! Hallelujah! Thank you Father God! Thank you Yeshua ha Messiach! Thank you Holy Spirit! Even if heaven were to be closed, there is no problem. We have already been seated with Him. If the enemy succeeded in closing the heavens, he would only be closing us in with the Father, the Son, and the Holy Spirit. The victory has been won! It can never be taken from us. Believe it! Receive it! Then live by the promise, and by faith take possession of it right now. Then hold on to it forever! Amen!

> *There is also an antitype which now saves us--baptism (not the removal of the filth of the flesh, but the answer of a good conscience toward God), through the resurrection of Jesus Christ, who has gone into heaven and is at the right hand of God, angels and authorities and powers having been made subject to Him* (1 Peter 3:21-22).

Everything has already been subjected to His power and authority. All powers and authorities in Heaven and on the Earth are subjected to His authority! Of course this does not mean that the Father is subject to Him. It is the Father who has given this to Him until the time when it is all given back as prophesied in the Word. But for now, Yeshua has it all!

I will say it again: As you receive this key, hold on to it with all your might. Never let it go. Remember that it is all about Yeshua! The Father has decreed it and it is awesome in our sight! Hear it again from Peter who was there when this promise was released! Hear it again from a faithful witness!

> *For He received from God the Father honor and glory when such a voice came to Him from the Excellent Glory: "This is My beloved Son, in whom I am well pleased." And we heard this voice which came from heaven when we were with Him on the holy mountain* (2 Peter 1:17-18).

PRAYER

I do not pray for these alone, but also for those who will believe in Me through their word; that they all may be one, as You, Father, are in Me, and I in You; that they also may be one in Us, that the world may believe that You sent Me. And the glory which You gave Me I have given them, that they may be one just as We are one: I in them, and You in Me; that they may be made perfect in one, and that the world may know that You have sent Me, and have loved them as You have loved Me. Father, I desire that they also whom You gave Me may be with Me where I am, that they may behold My glory which You have given Me; for You loved Me before the foundation of the world. O righteous Father! The world has not known You, but I have known You; and these have known that You sent Me. And I have declared to them Your name, and will declare it, that the love with which You loved Me may be in them, and I in them (John 17:20-26).

PAUSE AND REFLECT

1. In what ways did the resurrection of Yeshua change the attitude of the disciples?

2. In what ways has the resurrection changed your attitude about Yeshua?

3. How can you position yourself to receive and minister in "great grace?"

4. How has your relationship with Yeshua positioned you for an open heaven?

5. What Key to the Open Heaven is revealed in Ephesians 2:14-20?

CHAPTER 2

THE KINGDOM IS AT HAND

KEY 2: KNOWING HOW CLOSE IT IS

VISION REPORT: AUGUST 7, 2014

The power of God's presence continues to grow stronger each day! Are you feeling it? The Spirit of Wisdom and Revelation is working more powerfully and quickly as this season continues to open for us. Visions are coming quicker in worship. Prophetic dreams are more frequent and more powerful. Are you experiencing this too? The Lord is ready to do something amazing and powerful, and He is letting us know about it. Remember Amos 3:7, *"Surely the Lord God does nothing, unless He reveals His secret to His servants the prophets."* We must listen carefully for the revelations of the Lord in this season.

This morning, I began to see many visions of powerful things happening in the heavens. I saw dark clouds, rumbling storms and the fire of God moving powerfully in the Heavens. The fire of God was flashing powerfully from the East to the West. As I was watching all these signs in the Heavens, a portal suddenly opened. I understood from the Holy Spirit that we must remember that we are under an Open Heaven right now. We don't have to wait for it, but we do need to watch for it. My thoughts were directed by the Holy Spirit to Revelation, Chapter Nineteen.

Now I saw heaven opened, and behold, a white horse. And He who sat on him was called Faithful and True, and in righteousness He judges and makes war (Revelation 19:11).

We need to be ready for this season to open. In a vision, I looked intently into the portal opened into Heaven. As I focused on the Open Heaven, I was lifted up through it to a place I had never seen before. I was in what seemed like an open clearing in a deep and densely packed forest. As I looked around the area, I realized that I was in an outdoor training area. I noticed that this area was also a place of replenishing and resourcing from the Lord. I stood in the clearing pondering what this meant.

Suddenly the Lord gave me a vision within the vision. I started to see many faces which all looked very pleasant and very good. However, I soon learned that all was not as it seemed. The Lord was cautioning us not to be deceived by appearances. The Holy Spirit guided me to remember what Paul taught in the eleventh chapter of 2 Corinthians:

For such are false apostles, deceitful workers, transforming themselves into apostles of Christ. And no wonder! For Satan himself transforms himself into an angel of light. Therefore it is no great thing if his ministers also transform themselves into ministers of righteousness, whose end will be according to their works (2 Corinthians 11:13-15).

The Lord then told me that the deception of the world and of the enemy is very strong right now. It has been steadily growing in strength in these last days. However, the Lord was warning us that it is going to get even stronger. We must prepare now! We must be ready, NOW! Consider what you are doing to prepare. Are you ready? Are you waiting and watching for the signs of the times? Are you aware of the seasons of the Lord?

Then I saw something like banquet tables piled high with all kinds of nourishing and delicious looking foods. I quickly learned that this was about something in the Spirit. We need to earnestly seek to have our spirits nourished, replenished, and made strong if we are going to be ready for the next move of the Lord. We also need to get ready for all the ways the enemy will try to block this move of the Lord. He plans to disqualify and destroy as many of us as possible. It is a season to have a focused desire to live holy and pure lives. We must not relent from watching and waiting or the enemy will lull us to sleep and cover us with powerful deception. Remember Paul's instructions in Chapter One of the book of Colossians:

And you, who once were alienated and enemies in your mind by wicked works, yet now He has reconciled in the body of His flesh through death, to present you holy, and blameless, and above reproach in His sight—if indeed you continue in the faith, grounded and steadfast, and are not moved away from the hope of the gospel which you heard, which was preached to every creature under heaven, of which I, Paul, became a minister (Colossians 1:21-23).

The Lord is seeking those who will love Him, obey Him, and stand firm with Him! As the Holy Spirit spoke to me about these things, I spent some time in introspection. I wanted to know how well I am prepared for this new season of the Lord. I encourage you to do the same thing. There was a real urgency in all that the Lord was showing me in these visions. So, I will ask again: Are you ready to stand with the Lord in these last days? If not, then begin to prepare right now! Remember the time is short. My thoughts went to what Jesus said in Mark, Chapter Thirteen:

> *Jesus said to them: "Watch out that no one deceives you. Many will come in my name, claiming, 'I am he,' and will deceive many. When you hear of wars and rumors of wars, do not be alarmed. Such things must happen, but the end is still to come. Nation will rise against nation, and kingdom against kingdom. There will be earthquakes in various places, and famines. These are the beginning of birth pains"* (Mark 13:5-8).

These words from the Lord sound like the stories on every news program both on TV and on the internet today. Could we be experiencing these "birth pains" today? By showing you these things, the Lord is not trying to lead you into fear and anxiety. As you hear the Lord always remember that He does not give you a spirit of fear (2 Timothy 1:7, "*For God has not given us a spirit of fear, but of power and of love and of a sound mind.*") He is releasing love, power and soundness of mind to all His followers today. After arming you with these gifts of spiritual warfare, He is calling you to readiness. He is calling you to be watchful and prepared for what must come! I ask again: Are you ready for it?

I pray that you and I will be watchful and constantly praying for wisdom and revelation from the Lord! I am crying out for a greater anointing in the gifts of discerning in the spiritual realm! How about you? Remember what

Jesus said in Mark 13:37, *"What I say to you, I say to everyone: 'Watch!'"* Also remember Psalm 123:1-2 (The Message), *"I look to you, heaven-dwelling God, look up to you for help. Like servants, alert to their master's commands, like a maiden attending her lady, We're <u>watching</u> and <u>waiting</u>, holding our breath, awaiting your word of mercy."* I am watching and waiting! How about you? May the Lord wake us up and keep us alert! Amen!!!

The visions ended, but I am stilling feel a tingling of His power lingering in the air. I believe it is because something powerful is about to happen. I am praying for a greater anointing for discerning spiritual things. I am pursuing love and earnestly desiring spiritual gifts (1 Corinthians 14:1). I am seeking a greater ability to discern the spirits of God and to know more fully what He is doing and what He is about to release in this new season. (1 Corinthians 12:10, *"...to another discerning of spirits..."*) Something really powerful and awesome is about to break through in the spiritual realm. Are you feeling this too? I live daily in expectancy because I sense that time is short and the Lord is about to fulfill His greatest promises to us. I don't want to miss any of the things He is releasing!

(End of Vision Report)

FIRST ALERT: HEAVEN IS AT HAND

In those days John the Baptist came preaching in the wilderness of Judea, and saying, "Repent, for the kingdom of heaven is at hand" (Matthew 3:1-2)!

We have been warned! The warning has been sounded! The alert has been given! Those who are wise in the things of the Kingdom have taken note. They are working tirelessly to get ready and stay ready. The Lord has made known a mystery of the Kingdom. Heaven is so close that you can feel it! It is at hand! In other words, you can literally reach out and touch it. You can feel it in the natural, and sense it in the spiritual with your gifts of discerning the things of the Spirit.

Can you feel the closeness of the kingdom of God? At times, it seems so close that you can literally smell it. We have experienced this often during worship in recent weeks. As we move into our worship room, the fragrance of the Lord is there. I can often smell the burning incense on the golden altar as our prayers are lifted up to the Lord. As we walk around the house, we are touched by pockets filled with a very sweet fragrance. These are the fragrances of the Lord and of His holy angels. They are in our midst! This is not a far out idea or something I have dreamed up. You can see this idea clearly in the Word of God! Look again at 2 Corinthians, Chapter Two, and read it aloud until it becomes yours.

> *Now thanks be to God who always leads us in triumph in Christ, and through us diffuses the fragrance of His knowledge in every place. For we are to God the fragrance of Christ among those who are being saved and among those who are perishing. To the one we are the aroma of death leading to death, and to the other the aroma of life leading to life. And who is sufficient for these things? For we are not, as so many, peddling the word of God; but as of sincerity, but as from God, we speak in the sight of God in Christ* (2 Corinthians 2:14-17).

There is a fragrance associated with the knowledge of Yeshua ha Messiach. He still has that fragrance of all of the spices given to Him at His birth and those which covered Him in the tomb. There is a sweet, sweet fragrance which comes to us when He is near. Remember also the fragrance which was poured over Him before He went to the cross. "*Then Mary took a pound of very costly oil of spikenard, anointed the feet of Jesus, and wiped His feet with her hair. And the house was filled with the fragrance of the oil*" (John 12:3). Is your house filled with the fragrance of the Lord's presence? Wake up your anointing to see, hear, perceive, and smell the things of the Spirit! Amen?

The fragrances of all these spices are so powerful that they begin to get attached to us. Isn't that an awesome word from the Lord? Read Song of Solomon 1:3 aloud and receive this as a prophetic word for you: "*Because of the fragrance of your good ointments, Your name is ointment poured forth;*" The name, Yeshua, carries this powerful fragrance and He has put this ointment on us. I believe this is also a powerful spiritual truth about the robe of righteousness given to us by Yeshua. It has His fragrance on it and when we are covered by Him, we even smell like Him to the Father.

Angels have a very sweet fragrance and you can smell their aroma when they are near. I am praying that the Father will increase our spiritual senses in this season so that we can be more aware of what He is doing. I want to be able to use all of my God given senses to better understand what He is doing and where He is moving. The Lord is releasing an impartation of these spiritual gifts through the work of the Holy Spirit. If you want this, just open your spirit to receive it and claim it. Do this by making Word based decrees from your own mouth! We need all of these gifts to take our stand against the wiles of the devil in this season. Amen?

One of the great spiritual challenges for us will be to stay alert in this season. The challenge for remaining vigilant is faced by every army in the natural, and it is true for the armies of the Lord. While I was on active duty as an Army Chaplain many people wanted to tell me jokes about soldiers going to sleep on guard duty and then having the presence of mind to shout "Amen!" when they were caught by the Sergeant of the Guard. Of course every Sergeant of the Guard knew these stories and they were not easily fooled by the soldier's feeble attempts to avoid punishment. The Lord also knows all of our spiritual tricks. We can't fool Him! We must listen to Him, obey, and stay alert! Amen?

The truth is that people do tend to grow weary while waiting. It is difficult to stay focused over a long period of time. Many of us have heard about the coming of the kingdom most of our lives. Some are convinced that it could come any moment and they are staying alert. Others have grown weary, given up and turned away. We must not allow this to happen to us! We must thoroughly learn and put into practice the lesson given by Paul in Galatians 6:9, "*And let us not grow weary while doing good, for in due season we shall reap if we do not lose heart.*"

Harvest time is so close! I believe that we are now in the beginning of the great Harvest promised throughout the Word of God. We cannot afford to give up now! We will reap what we sow. If you are sowing to the Spirit, you will reap a spiritual harvest. If you are sowing to the flesh, you will reap the final judgment coming on the flesh. Read aloud the passage below! Read it over and over until it quickens your spirit to wake up and remain vigilant.

Do not be deceived, God is not mocked; for whatever a man sows, that he will also reap. For he who sows to his flesh will of the flesh reap corruption, but he who sows to the Spirit will of the Spirit reap everlasting life (Galatians 6:7-8).

There is a great reward for those who choose not to grow weary. There is a promise for those who are determined not to stumble and fall in this critical moment. Soldiers have developed many techniques to stay awake on guard duty. They play mental games, recite the lessons from their training, or search the area for hidden dangers. They do whatever it takes to stay alert so that they will not be caught sleeping when their leader returns. We need to develop that same loyalty and desire to please our leader, Yeshua ha Messiach! Amen? I pray that we will do whatever it takes to stay alert and watching for the Lord.

If we can trust the Lord a little more, we will be certain that He is the source of the strength, energy, and focus we need to obey His Word. He will provide above and beyond all we ask of Him. He will release things to us which are much greater than we have ever imagined. He is not trying to trick us! He is not trying to sneak up and catch us off guard! He is speaking clearly, directly and truthfully to all His disciples. Think about it! Look again at the promises of the Lord given in Isaiah, Chapter Forty:

Even youths grow tired and weary, and young men stumble and fall; but those who hope in the LORD will renew their strength. They will soar on wings like eagles; they will run and not grow weary, they will walk and not be faint (Isaiah 40:30-31, NIV).

If you need more strength, stamina or endurance, remember the Lord is faithful and He will provide all you need. In fact, He has already provided all you need. You just need to learn to see it and then to accept if by faith. We do this by reading the promises of the Lord over and over until they become perfectly real in our spirits and our souls. Think about what the writer of Hebrews is saying to you in this season.

Consider him who endured such opposition from sinful men, so that you will not grow weary and lose heart. In your struggle against sin, you have not yet resisted to the point of shedding your blood. And you have forgotten that word of encouragement that addresses you as sons: "My son, do not make light of the Lord's discipline, and do not lose heart when he rebukes you, because the Lord disciplines those he loves, and he punishes everyone he accepts as a son." Endure hardship as discipline; God is treating you as sons. For what son is not disciplined by his father (Hebrews 12:3-7, NIV)?

JESUS TOOK IT FURTHER

Jesus took this powerful promise from the Lord and extended it further than John had been able to do. It became a central part of His gospel of the Kingdom of God. *"From that time Jesus began to preach and to say, 'Repent, for the kingdom of heaven is at hand.'"* (Matthew 4:17) When Jesus proclaimed this message it was much deeper than with John. This is because Yeshua ha Messiach is the greatest carrier of the kingdom who ever walked on the face of the earth. He is the Key! He is the way, the truth, and the life, and He wants to bring all of God's children home to the Father!

Then Jesus said to them again, "Most assuredly, I say to you, I am the door of the sheep. All who ever came before Me are thieves and robbers, but the sheep did not hear them. I am the door. If anyone enters by Me, he will be saved, and will go in and out and find pasture. The thief does not come except to steal, and to kill, and to destroy. I have come that they may have life, and that they may have it more abundantly" (John 10:7-10).

Jesus did much more than just talk about the door. He is the door! Jesus did so much more than just talk about entering the Kingdom of God. He is the entrance. He promises that we can go in and out of the door. We have access to heaven right now, and we will live there with Him for all eternity. Jesus offers this powerful key to you. Jesus released an Open Heaven through a door that cannot be shut again.

You have been set free to move about the heavens! You can visit Him where He is and you can know Him for Who He is! Hallelujah! The Lord has done all of this for you and for me. Do you believe this? This is the critical question. You cannot receive what your faith cannot carry! It is time to strive to increase your most holy faith. Study the scriptures and take them into your heart. Remember, you do this by reading them aloud over and over until they become a part of you. This will build up your faith on the strong foundation of the Word of God.

That is the purpose of this book. I want to encourage and inspire you to seek the Open Heaven. I want you to get a firm grasp on the promises of God. I want you to be set free from the spirit of religion which tries to deceive you into believing that this is for someone else or for a different time. It is for you! It is for you right NOW! Just open your spirit to receive it. Seek to renew your mind so that your spirit can be transformed to carry all these powerful and wonderful promises from Father God. Jesus paid a huge price to bring these things to you. May you give Him everything He paid for on that horrible cross of suffering! Don't miss the promises and benefits of an Open Heaven now when it is so close and the time is so short!

JESUS SENDS US TO PREACH IT

As you truly open your spirit to the teaching of the Word and to the Spirit of wisdom and revelation, you find that it just keeps getting better and better. The Lord has not called you to sit on the sidelines and watch Him do all the work. He has called you to carry the kingdom of God in your heart and share these keys with others. He has not called you to sit in the stands and watch His team win the big game. He has called you to be a player on the field.

It is time to step out in faith to do what the Lord has called you to do for the Kingdom! Your participation is very important to the Lord and to your future. Hear the powerful and awesome command released by the Lord in Matthew 10:7, *"And as you go, preach, saying, 'The kingdom of heaven is at hand.'"* The Lord is assuming that you will go. The question is: What will you do as you go? Will you proclaim the Kingdom? Will you tell people how close it is? Will you share with them the keys to an Open Heaven?

Every true believer has been called to preach the Gospel of the Kingdom. This does not necessarily mean that you have been called to be a pastor in a church; although you might be. The primary calling is to spread the gospel. You can do that with any occupation if you are willing to be a Kingdom carrier. You can speak powerful prophetic words into the lives of those you meet in the marketplace and in your own neighborhood.

How do you do this? You must have the Gospel of the Kingdom planted so deeply and so powerfully in your heart that it spills over wherever you are and to whom ever you are speaking. How do you receive this? You read aloud all the promises of the Word. Read them over and over as you let them take root in your heart. Every word you speak from your mouth goes into your heart and becomes part of who you are. Are you ready for it? Listen to the Word of the Lord once more: Matthew 10:7, *"And as you go, preach, saying, 'The kingdom of heaven is at hand.'"*

JESUS ENCOURAGES US TO PRESS INTO IT

This is not a time to sit quietly by and watch others do what the Lord has commanded. The calling has been given to you and to everyone who believes in Yeshua ha Messiach. The anointing is for everyone who is born again and baptized with the Holy Spirit and with fire. The commissioning has been released to all disciples. How will you answer the Lord in this season? I love the imagery of the baptism of the Holy Spirit in Acts, Chapter Two.

Then there appeared to them divided tongues, as of fire, and one sat upon each of them. And they were all filled with the Holy Spirit and began to speak with other tongues, as the Spirit gave them utterance (Acts 2:3-4).

They were all set on fire by the Lord so that they could move in the power He was making available to them. I pray that He is setting you on fire right now for the same purpose. Those newly baptized disciples rushed out into the streets of Jerusalem. What else could they do? What would you do if your hair had been set on fire by the Lord? You cannot sit by and watch when you have a fire on your head. The fire of the Lord inspires you to take action and to take it quickly. On the Day of Pentecost, the believers were not rushing out to find something to extinguish the fire as so many do today. They rushed out so they could set more people on fire for the Lord.

Perhaps the Lord needed to do this to energize them to fully move in what He had released earlier. In Matthew 11:12, He said, *"And from the days of John the Baptist until now the kingdom of heaven suffers violence, and the violent take it by force."* When you are on fire, you will do some violent things. Perhaps you need to rekindle that fire so that you can be filled again with the zeal of the Lord to spread the Gospel. May the fire of God come on you over and over so that you can never grow weary in the work of the Kingdom!

Unbelieving people in the world are living in deep darkness. The enemy has covered the world with his thick veil of deception. He is the one who wants to bring darkness rather than light to everyone on planet Earth. But we are not of the kingdom of darkness. We are of the kingdom of light. Remember the promise release in Isaiah, Chapter Sixty:

> *Arise, shine; for your light has come! And the glory of the Lord is risen upon you. For behold, the darkness shall cover the earth, and deep darkness the people; but the Lord will arise over you, and His glory will be seen upon you. The Gentiles shall come to your light, and kings to the brightness of your rising* (Isaiah 60:1-3).

Father God did this amazing thing for us through Yeshua ha Messiach. Remember what He said in John 9:5, *"As long as I am in the world, I am the light of the world."* That promise was fulfilled and that light came into the world, but tragically people didn't recognize it. They missed that window of opportunity which the Lord had opened for them. Heaven was torn open, but they didn't have a heart to perceive it, eyes to see it, or ears to hear it.

The Lord didn't leave people in that sad situation. The Lord has good news for you. It is fresh and new every day. He has more good news for the world, and He is releasing it right now. This news is also for you and for me. There is still hope! The window of opportunity has not been slammed shut! The torn Heaven has not been sown shut! The light is still here both for and in those who believe in Yeshua ha Messiach. Believe what Jesus decreed:

> *You are the light of the world. A city that is set on a hill cannot be hidden. Nor do they light a lamp and put it under a basket, but on a lampstand, and it gives light to all who are in the house. Let your light so shine before men, that they may see your good works and glorify your Father in heaven* (Matthew 5:14-16).

Now it is your turn! This is your season to carry the light! It is like a great relay race for all time. One generation passes the baton to the next. If each generation is faithful to their calling, the baton will never be dropped. The next generation will not be lost if the faithful in this season carry it to them and release it through the Holy Spirit. Whether they know it or not, the next generation is depending on you. Don't let them down. Carry it to them as quickly as possible. Pass the Kingdom Keys to the next generation!

I pray that the Lord will set you on fire so that you will become the "light of the world." It is His fire and it is His light, but He has called you and me to carry it. Are you ready for your season in the Lord? Are you ready to step out in your anointing and be all that the Lord has called you to be? Be the light of the world! Be a carrier of the fire! Be a messenger of God releasing the gospel of the Kingdom to everyone you meet wherever you go! Amen?

PRAYER

I pray for them. I do not pray for the world but for those whom You have given Me, for they are Yours. And all Mine are Yours, and Yours are Mine, and I am glorified in them. Now I am no longer in the world, but these are in the world, and I come to You. Holy Father, keep through Your name those whom You have given Me, that they may be one as We are. While I was with them in the world, I kept them in Your name. Those whom You gave Me I have kept; and none of them is lost except the son of perdition, that the Scripture might be fulfilled. But now I come to You, and these things I speak in the world, that they may have My joy fulfilled in themselves. I have given them Your word; and the world has hated them because they are not of the world, just as I am not of the world. I do not pray that You should take them out of the world, but that You should keep them from the evil one. They are not of the world, just as I am not of the world. Sanctify them by Your truth. Your word is truth. As You sent Me into the world, I also have sent them into the world (John 17:9-18).

PAUSE AND REFLECT

1. What are you doing to prepare for the next season of the Lord?

2. Which of the things in the last paragraph of the vision report are you doing to prepare?

3. In what ways have you felt the closeness of the kingdom of God?

4. In what ways is the Lord using fragrance to lead you to an open heaven experience?

5. What steps are you ready to take in order to stay alert and ready?

6. What can you do to open your spiritual eyes to see the open heaven?

7. "You cannot receive what your faith cannot carry!" What does this mean to you?

8. What are you doing to spread the Gospel of the Kingdom?

CHAPTER 3

SEEING AN OPEN HEAVEN

KEY 3: OPEN YOUR EYES AND SEE

(THEN KEEP THEM OPEN)

As a believer and disciple of Jesus Christ, you are not alone and helpless. You are not powerless in your life and work for the Kingdom of God. It is time to stand in the authority the Lord has given (Luke 10:19, "*Behold, I give you the authority to trample on serpents and scorpions, and over all the power of the enemy, and nothing shall by any means hurt you.*") and in the power of His might (Ephesians 6:10, "*Finally, my brethren, be strong in the Lord and in the power of His might.*"). It is time for us to take authority over our own spirits and begin to release our spiritual gifts in the fullness of the Lord. Remember what Paul wrote in 1 Corinthians 14:32, "*And the spirits of the prophets are subject to the prophets.*" Your spirit is subject to you! It is time to begin to speak in authority over your own spirit and wake up all your spiritual gifts. Begin even now to stir up the gifts of God which were released to you through the laying on of hands.

Therefore I remind you to stir up the gift of God which is in you through the laying on of my hands. For God has not given us a spirit of fear, but of power and of love and of a sound mind (2 Timothy 1:6-7).

Now is the time to stir up your seer anointing. It has been limited or dormant long enough! Amen? Heaven's mysteries have been revealed and the Lord wants you to see them. The best definition of a Biblical mystery is: something formerly hidden which has now been made visible to Spirit-led believers. Stir up your seer gift right now! In the NIV, Paul's instruction about activating your spiritual gifts is translated as "fan into flame." I don't know about you, but I am fanning the gifts as intensely as I can. I don't want to let my spiritual eyes be so closed that I cannot see the mysteries of the Kingdom which the Lord has clearly made manifest to all His true disciples.

He answered and said to them, "Because it has been given to you to know the mysteries of the kingdom of heaven, but to them it has not been given. For whoever has, to him more will be given, and he will have abundance; but whoever does not have, even what he has will be taken away from him" (Matthew 13:11-12).

This is an awesome gift from the Lord. "*...it has been given to you to know the mysteries of the kingdom...*" I am so thankful to the Lord for revealing the deep things of the Spirit to us, and I want to receive everything He is giving. I want to have my spiritual eyes wide open to see. How about you? Begin now to speak to your spirit and command it to open your spiritual eyes! Remember your spirit is subject to you! Don't let another day go by with spiritual blindness blocking you from your inheritance in the Lord!

KEYS TO HEAVEN HAVE BEEN REVEALED

And I also say to you that you are Peter, and on this rock I will build My church, and the gates of Hades shall not prevail against it. And I will give you the keys of the kingdom of heaven, and whatever you bind on earth will be bound in heaven, and whatever you loose on earth will be loosed in heaven (Matthew 16:18-19).

Jesus gave the keys to the kingdom to Peter first. Some people seem to be very content to just know this fact. However, I am not content to know that something was given hundreds of years ago which does not apply to me. I believe that every promise in the Bible is for you and for me. I claim the keys to the kingdom which were given to Peter. How about you? These keys were given to the entire Body of Christ. As part of that body, they are also for me! Amen?

We visit Israel every year. When we are in Capernaum, I like to go over to a very large statue of Peter. The statue of Peter has the shepherd's staff and a set of kingdom keys. I always speak to Peter and say, "Peter, you don't seem to be using those keys right now! Please give them to me! I will use them!" This may sound silly to some people, but I believe we can activate spiritual things by speaking them into being. I don't want to miss even one opportunity to get hold of those kingdom keys. How about you?

Having these kingdom keys is not something which should give us any spiritual pride. We haven't earned the keys. They are not given because we are good enough. They are given because of what Yeshua ha Messiach did for us on the cross of Calvary! When we accept these keys, we are simply being obedient to follow His commands and continue to do His work on Earth! In fact, humility is the key to operating in the fullness of this gift from the Lord.

> *Then Jesus called a little child to Him, set him in the midst of them, and said, "Assuredly, I say to you, unless you are converted and become as little children, you will by no means enter the kingdom of heaven. Therefore whoever humbles himself as this little child is the greatest in the kingdom of heaven"* (Matthew 18:2-4).

A child simply trusts the Lord to do what He says he is going to do. A child takes the gifts and shows gratitude to the giver. A child knows that he did not create the key or earn it by good works. A child knows how to receive a gift and simply enjoy what the Lord has done. That is what the Lord is asking us to do. Become as trusting as a small child and show Yeshua the gratitude He so richly deserves.

He has given these awesome spiritual gifts and opened the Heavens for us. He has done this so that we can see and do what the Father is doing. He has done this so that we can hear and speak what the Father is saying. We can't do that unless we have access to the Father in Heaven. The only way we can have that access is as a gift of God delivered by the Holy Spirit. We must always remember that it is all about Him!

FIRST MANIFESTATION OF OPEN HEAVEN

As I started my search of the Scriptures to better under-stand the reality of an open Heaven, I wanted to find the first instances of it happening. I believe that Jacob was the first to experience the fullness of this blessing. He wasn't seeking it or crying out for it. The Lord simply gave

Him a beautiful experience of His provision and protection which was being made available by His grace. The passage below is loaded with revelation about the Open Heaven. I recommend that you read it over and over as you seek revelation from the Lord for a full understanding of what it means for you.

> *Now Jacob went out from Beersheba and went toward Haran. So he came to a certain place and stayed there all night, because the sun had set. And he took one of the stones of that place and put it at his head, and he lay down in that place to sleep. Then he dreamed, and behold, a ladder was set up on the earth, and its top reached to heaven; and there the angels of God were ascending and descending on it. And behold, the LORD stood above it and said: "I am the LORD God of Abraham your father and the God of Isaac; the land on which you lie I will give to you and your descendants. Also your descendants shall be as the dust of the earth; you shall spread abroad to the west and the east, to the north and the south; and in you and in your seed all the families of the earth shall be blessed. Behold, I am with you and will keep you wherever you go, and will bring you back to this land; for I will not leave you until I have done what I have spoken to you." Then Jacob awoke from his sleep and said, "Surely the LORD is in this place, and I did not know it." And he was afraid and said, "How awesome is this place! This is none other than the house of God, and this is the gate of heaven"* (Genesis 28:10-17)!

Did you notice that Jacob first saw the angels ascending to Heaven? What is this saying to you? It is clear that the angels were already there, but he had not been able to see them. The Lord opened his spiritual eyes so that he could see that he had not been alone on his journey. Angels were already assigned to assist and protect him. After their missions were completed, they ascended back to Heaven. Then Jacob saw that other angels were descending. What does this say to you? The Lord is sending more angels to minister His gifts in accordance with His will.

This same gift of seeing in the spiritual realm is available to you and to me. The Lord has released angels to go with us and minister His gifts and grace to us. We are not alone! We have not been abandoned or left without the Lord's presence. Whether we can see it or not, the angels are all around us. Wouldn't it be better if you could see them and cooperate with them in their work? Well, you can!

Continue to wake up your seer anointing! Continue to stir up your spiritual gifts! Continue to fan them into a flame so that the fire of God can burn away the scales over your eyes. Activate the gifts so that you can see through every veil of deception the enemy has sent to block you! Amen? This is a gift from the Lord and He has given you the spiritual authority to activate it and increase it.

If this was all that Jacob saw, it would be enough. But, the Lord had so much more for him, and He has so much more for you! As Jacob's eyes looked higher and higher up the ladder into Heaven, He saw something truly awesome. He saw the Lord standing at the top of the ladder. Does your heart long to see the Lord? Are you seeking His face? Are you a part of the generation of Jacob?

Who may ascend into the hill of the Lord? Or who may stand in His holy place? He who has clean hands and a pure heart, who has not lifted up his soul to an idol, nor sworn deceitfully. He shall receive blessing from the Lord, and righteousness from the God of his salvation. This is Jacob, the generation of those who seek Him, who seek Your face (Psalm 24:3-6).

This experience changed Jacob's life forever, and meeting the Lord of the Open Heaven will do the same for you. To Jacob this seemed to be "the house of God" and "the gate of heaven." He thought there was something special about the place. He didn't have a mentor or study resources to help him understand what he was experiencing. On the other hand, you have all these things available to you. You also have the Spirit of Truth to guide you into all truth. You can understand that the Open Heaven is available to you wherever you may be. You can actually carry the Open Heaven with you and experience it daily. You can have access to the angels of the Lord and see the Lord in all of your walk with Him. Hallelujah! Thank you Lord!

After spending time reflecting on the meaning of Jacob's experience and claiming it for myself, I began to seek to understand what the Lord is providing for His people through the Open Heaven. What do the angels bring to us? What are they going back to Heaven to receive and bring back to you and to me right now? I searched the Scriptures to see the things the Lord has given in the past. This is always a great clue as to what the Lord is doing right now. Some of the things I discovered are listed below.

HEAVEN OPENED TO RELEASE FOOD FOR THE PEOPLE

Then the LORD said to Moses, "Behold, I will rain bread from heaven for you. And the people shall go out and gather a certain quota every day, that I may test them, whether they will walk in My law or not" (Exodus 16:4).

What does this say to you? Is there a promise in this move of the Lord which is also for you and for me? I always believe that every promise and gift of the Lord in the Word is also available to me! I believe them and receive them by faith as soon as they manifest in the Word. I know that the Lord is releasing a promise to me in this passage. What is it saying to you?

To me the Lord is releasing a powerful promise of provision to meet every need. He is "Jehovah-Jireh," the Lord who provides. We see the Lord as our provider as Abraham saw Him in Genesis 22:14 *"And Abraham called the name of the place, The-Lord-Will-Provide; as it is said to this day, 'In the Mount of the Lord it shall be provided.'"* Remember that the Lord is the same yesterday, today and forever (Hebrews 13:8). Remember that we are the heirs to the blessing of Abraham as decreed in Galatians, Chapter Three:

Christ has redeemed us from the curse of the law, having become a curse for us (for it is written, "Cursed is everyone who hangs on a tree"), that the blessing of Abraham might come upon the Gentiles in Christ Jesus, that we might receive the promise of the Spirit through faith (Galatians 3:13-14).

The things He provided for Abraham, He will provide for you! The gifts He gave to Jacob, He will provide for you! Everything He promised in the past is still available to His followers today. Do you believe that? Think about it as you read these passages of scripture. Then decree aloud:

"The provisions of the Lord for Abraham and Yeshua are available for me and for you today!" Amen!

THE LORD SPEAKS FROM HEAVEN

Then the LORD said to Moses, "Thus you shall say to the children of Israel: You have seen that I have talked with you from heaven" (Exodus 20:22).

All of the people of Israel heard the awesome voice of the Lord spoken from Heaven. They didn't respond well to that experience. It caused them to fear Him and draw back from Him. They knew how sinful they were. They believed that the Lord would kill them if they came near to Him. So, they were content to let Moses go into His presence and then bring the Word of the Lord back to them. Don't be content with someone else's experience with the Lord! Seek Him for yourself!

Out of heaven He let you hear His voice, that He might instruct you; on earth He showed you His great fire, and you heard His words out of the midst of the fire. And because He loved your fathers, therefore He chose their descendants after them; and He brought you out of Egypt with His Presence, with His mighty power, driving out from before you nations greater and mightier than you, to bring you in, to give you their land as an inheritance, as it is this day. Therefore know this day, and consider it in your heart, that the LORD Himself is God in heaven above and on the earth beneath; there is no other (Deuteronomy 4:36-39).

Will we make the same mistake? I don't know about you, but I cherish hearing the voice of the Lord from

Heaven. We do not need to fear, because we come before Him with the covering of Yeshua's blood. We come with the covering of His righteousness so that we can enter into His presence, hear His voice, and be enlivened and empowered to do His will. Seek the Open Heaven so that you can hear the voice of the Lord!

Seeing then that we have a great High Priest who has passed through the heavens, Jesus the Son of God, let us hold fast our confession. For we do not have a High Priest who cannot sympathize with our weaknesses, but was in all points tempted as we are, yet without sin. Let us therefore come boldly to the throne of grace, that we may obtain mercy and find grace to help in time of need (Hebrews 4:14-16).

GOD'S FIRE COMES DOWN FROM HEAVEN

Then you came near and stood at the foot of the mountain, and the mountain burned with fire to the midst of heaven, with darkness, cloud, and thick darkness (Deuteronomy 4:11).

That day the people were afraid of the fire of God. They passed up the amazing opportunity to ascend the mountain with Moses. They believed that they were safer in the doorway of their tents than on the Mountain of the Lord. They didn't think their hands were clean enough to be in His presence. They didn't believe that the condition of their hearts were pure enough to experience His power. They said "No!" to one of the most awesome invitations in the history of the World. That invitation was never given to them again.

Here is the good news! That invitation which was given to the Children of Israel has also been given to you. You can be made ready to ascend the hill of the Lord. You are made clean by the blood of Jesus. You can wear His robe of righteousness (Isaiah 61:10, *"For He has clothed me with the garments of salvation, He has covered me with the robe of righteousness"*). You have been made fireproof by the blood of Yeshua, and you can take the heat. This is another one of those Open Heaven promises which is available to you and to me. I don't want to miss it! How about you? Even now begin to ascend the Hill of the Lord! Bravely step through the fire and come boldly before the throne of His grace!

HEAVEN IS NEAR!

Many people ask me how they can make that extremely long journey to the Third Heaven. How far away is Heaven? What do you think? As I continued my search for the Open Heaven, I began to realize that Heaven is not at some infinitely great distance from Earth. That is an Old Testament way of thinking. We have a new covenant which makes it clear that Heaven is very close. This idea was first announced by John the Baptist.

In those days John the Baptist came preaching in the wilderness of Judea, and saying, "Repent, for the kingdom of heaven is at hand" (Matthew 3:1-2)!

Most believers just read this without really thinking it through. This was an amazing and wonderful revelation in John's day. People had never heard this idea before and they must have been stunned by John's assertion. Most of the people in John's day heard this as if John was speaking about time rather than distance. I believe that it is a prophecy about both time and distance. You no longer have to think about a distant Heaven which is

58

inaccessible to you. You also know that the fullness of the final manifestation of the Kingdom will come very soon.

Jesus picked up where John left off. *"From that time Jesus began to preach and to say, 'Repent, for the kingdom of heaven is at hand.'"* (Matthew 4:17) This could also be understood as speaking about time or distance as could the instructions given to the disciples in Matthew 10:7, *"And as you go, preach, saying, 'The kingdom of heaven is at hand.'"* A little later, Jesus made it clear when he said, *"And from the days of John the Baptist until now the kingdom of heaven suffers violence, and the violent take it by force."* (Matthew 11:12) If you can press into it right now, it means that it is close in both time and distance. Are you pressing in to the Open Heaven? Are you preaching that the kingdom of heaven is at hand? It is time for us to get on board with the Lord and be Open Heaven carriers and Open Heaven ministers!

SEERS BEGIN TO SEE THE LORD ON HIS THRONE

Then Micaiah said, "Therefore hear the word of the LORD: I saw the LORD sitting on His throne, and all the host of heaven standing by, on His right hand and on His left. And the LORD said, 'Who will per-suade Ahab to go up, that he may fall at Ramoth Gilead?' So one spoke in this manner, and another spoke in that manner. Then a spirit came forward and stood before the LORD, and said, 'I will per-suade him.' The LORD said to him, 'In what way?' So he said, 'I will go out and be a lying spirit in the mouth of all his prophets.' And the LORD said, 'You shall persuade him, and also prevail. Go out and do so'" (1 Kings 22:19-22).

In addition to Micaiah, we read about Isaiah, Daniel, Ezekiel, and John seeing the Lord on His throne. In 2 Corinthians, Chapter Twelve, Verse Two, Paul tells about a man who was caught up into the third Heaven. Jesus speaks of seeing the things the Father is doing and it is clear that He is seeing the Lord on His throne. David and Solomon wrote about the throne in such great detail that it is difficult to believe they had not actually seen it in their meetings with the Lord. Think about it! This isn't so strange after all.

SEEING WHERE AND HOW GOD IS SEATED

We need to quit thinking about the Open Heaven being some strange and alien idea. We are challenged to go boldly before the throne of the Lord in Hebrews 4:16. This is a good time to release your seer anointing in order to experience all that the Lord is opening for you right now. Amen? Begin to believe for it and expect it to manifest for you! Stand in faith and make decrees which will allow you to experience the Open Heaven!

> *O LORD of hosts, God of Israel, the One who dwells between the cherubim, You are God, You alone, of all the kingdoms of the earth. You have made heaven and earth* (Isaiah 37:16).

As you study these passages of Scripture, I encourage you to see how these visions of the Lord begin to enhance and increase the awe (fear) of the Lord. Remember Psalm 111:10, *"The fear of the LORD is the beginning of wisdom; a good understanding have all those who do His command-ments. His praise endures forever."* As you experience more of the holy fear of the Lord your understanding will be increased. It is a promise! I receive all these promises of the Lord. How about you? To prepare yourself for these experiences read Ezekiel, Chapter 1 as if it is your first time to see it. Try to get the intense feeling of Ezekiel into your own heart as if you are the one seeing this. Can you feel the intense awe and the pure fear of the Lord in His holy presence? Then study and meditate on Ezekiel's experiences revealed in the eighth chapter.

Then I looked, and there was a likeness, like the appearance of fire--from the appearance of His waist and downward, fire; and from His waist and upward, like the appearance of brightness, like the color of amber. He stretched out the form of a hand, and took me by a lock of my hair; and the Spirit lifted me up between earth and heaven, and brought me in visions of God to Jerusalem, to the door of the north gate of the inner court, where the seat of the image of jealousy was, which provokes to jealousy. And behold, the glory of the God of Israel was there, like the vision that I saw in the plain (Ezekiel 8:2-4).*

IS THIS REALLY FOR YOU AND ME?

And He said to him (Nathaniel), "Most assuredly, I say to you, hereafter you shall see heaven open, and the angels of God ascending and descending upon the Son of Man" (John 1:51).

We don't often think of Nathaniel as a seer. Yet, on their first meeting, the Lord decreed that Nathaniel would see Heaven open. Jesus proclaimed that Nathaniel would see angels ascending and descending. I love the way the Lord said it so clearly, "you shall see." In my spirit, I am hearing The Lord saying to you right now, "You shall see!" Do you believe it? Then say aloud, "I shall see!" Speak this into being in your own spirit. Begin to wake up you seer anointing.

What do you want to see? Perhaps you want to see angels. Then begin to let your confession be in agreement with Jesus. Speak aloud, "I shall see angels ascending and descending!" Now, let's take it up another notch! Would you like to see Jesus? That was the promise Jesus gave to Nathaniel. He was going to see more than just angels at work. He was going to see "the Son of Man." He was going to see all of this manifesting on Yeshua ha Messiach! Would you like to have this same kind of awesome spiritual experience? Then believe it and receive it by faith. Confess it with your mouth. Say aloud right now, "I shall see angels ascending and descending on the Son of Man!"

Look at it another way! What does Jesus want you to see? Clearly, He wants and expects His followers to experience what Nathaniel was going to see. He wants it for you too. Jesus wants you to see Heaven OPEN! He wants you to see the angels ascending and descending on Him. He also wants you to see even more. He wants you to see in the spiritual realm what is happening and what is moving right now.

Remember what He said in John 4:35, *"Don't you have a saying, its still four months until harvest? I tell you, open your eyes and look at the fields! They are ripe for harvest."* Jesus is saying to you today, "open your eyes and look!" Jesus wants you to see the fields which are ripe for harvest so that you can join in the work. I want you to remember that all the promises and gifts given to the disciples are also for you. Read the passage below over and over until it is yours. Read it aloud if possible. Claim Jesus' prayer for you own life and ministry.

I do not pray for these alone, but also for those who will believe in Me through their word; that they all may be one, as You, Father, are in Me, and I in You; that they also may be one in Us, that the world may believe that You sent Me. And the glory which You gave Me I have given them, that they may be one just as We are one: I in them, and You in Me; that they may be made perfect in one, and that the world may know that You have sent Me, and have loved them as You have loved Me (John 17:20-23).

Always remember that Jesus wants you to see spiritual truth. One of His most frequent statements was, "Let those who have eyes see!" He created you with both spiritual and physical eyes. You need to have both sets of eyes open to function fully in His anointing. But catch this, He tells you to open your own eyes. Who else can open them? We need to stop waiting for the Lord to do something and step out and take hold of what He has already given us.

I want to see what Jesus wants me to see. How about you? Then, open your eyes in accordance with Jesus' word. Right now, speak to your spiritual eyes: "Spiritual eyes open wide now!" Remember that the spirit of the prophet is subject to the prophet. You have authority over you own spirit, soul, and body. You are not a helpless victim or the pawn in some great cosmic battle. You are a disciple of Jesus Christ with all the authority and power you need to accomplish your mission for Him. Read aloud again the words of Jesus in Luke 10:19, "*Behold, I give you the authority to trample on serpents and scorpions, and over all the power of the enemy, and nothing shall by any means hurt you.*" Believe it with all your heart and confess it aloud every single day! Amen?

I want to receive everything the Lord is releasing right now! How about you? Say aloud, "I want to receive everything The Lord has for me!" How do you do that? Well, I asked The Lord, "How can we do that?" It is just that simple. He is not keeping secrets from us or withholding truth when we need it most. He is good all the time! He is so good right now that you can ask anything in His name! Amen? If you haven't been doing this already, ask for it right now.

I am totally ready to receive more! I am always ready to receive more from the Lord! How about you? Then say it aloud, "I'm ready to receive more!" Are we in agreement? Remember, there is great power in agreement. Remember what Jesus said in Matthew 18:19-20, "*Again I say to you that if two of you agree on earth concerning anything that they ask, it will be done for them by My Father in heaven. For where two or three are gathered together in My name, I am there in the midst of them.*" Do you believe this? Then it is time to act on your beliefs.

THE SEER ANOINTING

Do you have a seer anointing? It is important to understand that seers are anointed! However, too many people use this as an excuse to remain on the sidelines because they believe this is only for some kind of super-apostle. Yet, from the words of Jesus to Nathaniel, it seems clear to me that all believers should be seers. The missing ingredient is our willingness to believe it and receive it. It seems appropriate to ask, Who anoints the seers? Who can receive the anointing? In the next few paragraphs, I want to clear this up for you.

First, let's look at some very basic information about the seer anointing. There are at least two levels of anointing! Some of the confusion comes when we mix up the two positions. First there is the office of the Seer. Those receiving this anointing are chosen by the Holy Spirit. They are chosen for a very specific purpose and sometimes for a very specific and limited season. Holding this office can be very challenging. Many people do not want to hear what the Lord is saying to them or about them. They may lash out at the seer in anger or retribution. They may launch an attack on the seer in order to discredit and seriously damage the person holding this office. The Jezebel spirit is a specialist in these kinds of attacks. See my book, "A Warrior's Guide to the Seven Spirits of God, Part 1, Basic Training," for a full explanation of the work of this demonic spirit.

There are diversities of gifts, but the same Spirit. There are differences of ministries, but the same Lord. And there are diversities of activities, but it is the same God who works all in all. But the manifestation of the Spirit is given to each one for the profit of all: for to one is given the word of wisdom through the Spirit, to another the word of knowledge through the same Spirit, to another faith by the same Spirit, to another gifts of healings by the same Spirit, to another the working of miracles, to another prophecy, to another discerning of spirits, to another different kinds of tongues, to another the interpretation of tongues. But one and the same Spirit works all these things, distributing to each one individually as He wills (1 Corinthians 12:4-11).

You may or may not be in the office of the seer (prophet). Yet, you can still be a seer because there is a specific spiritual gift of seeing. Who can have this gift? I believe that it is available to every Spirit-filled believer. The Lord wants all of us to see and discern in the spiritual realm. Peter made this very clear on the Day of Pentecost when he declared that the prophecy given through Joel was being fulfilled in those who received the outpouring of the Holy Spirit.

> *But Peter, standing up with the eleven, raised his voice and said to them, "Men of Judea and all who dwell in Jerusalem, let this be known to you, and heed my words. For these are not drunk, as you suppose, since it is only the third hour of the day. But this is what was spoken by the prophet Joel: And it shall come to pass in the last days, says God, That I will pour out of My Spirit on all flesh; Your sons and your daughters shall prophesy, Your young men shall see visions, Your old men shall dream dreams. And on My menservants and on My maidservants I will pour out My Spirit in those days; And they shall prophesy. I will show wonders in heaven above and signs in the earth beneath: Blood and fire and vapor of smoke"* (Acts 2:14-19).

JESUS WAS A SEER

Have you ever thought of Jesus as a Seer? *"And no one has ascended to heaven except the One Who descended from Heaven, the Son of Man."* **(**John 3:13, ONMB) Jesus had Third Heaven visits. That's where He saw what the Father was doing. That is where He heard what the Father was saying. This was evidently a routine practice for Jesus.

> *Then Jesus answered and said to them, "Most assuredly, I say to you, the Son can do nothing of Himself, but what He sees the Father do; for what-ever He does, the Son also does in like manner.*

For the Father loves the Son, and shows Him all things that He Himself does; and He will show Him greater works than these, that you may marvel. For as the Father raises the dead and gives life to them, even so the Son gives life to whom He will" (John 5:19-21).

Have you noticed that Jesus could see people before He met them? When Jesus used His seer anointing, He saw far beyond mere physical appearance. He saw what they were doing inwardly. He saw their character. He even knew what they were thinking. In other words He saw them spirit, soul, and body. This has happened to me many times. It is not something I am able to do, but the Holy Spirit works this through me. He is also willing to work this through you! Remember we are supposed to do what Jesus did. He knew people from seeing them in the Spirit, and we should do the same thing.

"How do you know me?" Nathanael asked. Jesus answered, "I saw you while you were still under the fig tree before Philip called you." Then Nathanael declared, "Rabbi, you are the Son of God; you are the king of Israel" (John 1:48-49).

How do we prepare ourselves for something like this? This is so far beyond what most of us have been taught to believe and expect. Yet, it is clearly documented in the Scriptures. It is also being experienced by more and more people. Many people are receiving what was prophesied by Joel and released on the Day of Pentecost. If you have flesh, this is for you. Peter and Joel said that the Lord was releasing it on "all flesh."

But, where do we begin in our search to experience these things. I believe that the first step in being enabled to see the kingdom is to be born again. I recommend that you meditate on what Jesus said in John 3:3, "*Jesus answered and said to him, 'Most assuredly, I say to you, unless one is born again, he cannot see the kingdom of God.'*" Jesus is very clear on this topic. If you have not been born again, this is the time for you to allow the Lord to do this work in you. Then you will be enabled to see the Kingdom! Amen?

I don't believe that we have fully moved into this level of anointing, but it is clearly time for us to go to a higher level of Glory. Jesus promised that some of those who were following Him would see the Kingdom of God. There is a challenge in this for us. I don't want to be among those who do not see. How about you? I want to see everything the Lord is willing to reveal about the kingdom of God. Just a few days after making this promise, the Lord fulfilled it for three of the disciples. Peter, John and Jacob (James) saw the open Heaven, the cloud of glory, Moses, and Elijah. They heard the voice of Father God proclaiming who Jesus is and declaring Him as the chosen one.

And it was about eight days after these messages, and taking Peter and John and Jacob He went up to the mountain to pray for Himself. And it happened while He was praying, the appearance of His face was different and His cloak (prayer shawl) was white, gleaming like lightning. And behold, two men were speaking with Him, who were Moses and Elijah, while those who had been seen in glory were speaking about His death, which He was going to fulfill in Jerusalem. And Peter and those with him were burdened in sleep; but as they kept awake, they saw His glory and the two men who had stood with Him. Then it happened while they were being separate from Him, Peter said to Y'shua, "Master, it is good for us to be here, now let us make three booths: one for You, and one for Moses, and one for Elijah" although he had not understood what he was saying. But while he was saying these things a cloud came and covered them; and they were afraid while they entered the cloud. Then a voice came from the cloud saying, "This is My Son, the one Who has been chosen, you must continually listen to Him" (Luke 9:28-35, ONMB)!

Think about these verses from Luke, Chapter Nine as they apply to this glory manifestation! Think about what these things mean for you and for me! They were made manifest to a group of men we might call Jesus' Inner Circle (Peter, James and John). I want to be in that inner circle! How about you? I want to see and hear what the Lord is doing and saying. Can we do that? If we really trust Jesus and believe what He said, it is possible. Meditate again on what Jesus said. Speak it out loud until it sinks deeply into your heart and your faith.

Most assuredly, I say to you, he who believes in Me, the works that I do he will do also; and greater works than these he will do, because I go to My Father. And whatever you ask in My name, that I will do, that the Father may be glorified in the Son. If you ask anything in My name, I will do it (John 14:12-14).

Do you believe this? Most Christians say that they believe it, but they don't live it. I have thought about this many times. I came to the conclusion that what people are really saying is that they believe Jesus said it. However, they don't really believe that it is the truth for them. If you are one of the few – one of the chosen – who truly believes what Jesus said and if you know that it is for you, then it is time to do some greater works.

Jesus taught that all we need to do is ask. So, why not ask right now? Pray aloud, "Lord help me to do the greater works! Help me to believe it and to receive it!" If you are really doing this, you may be ready to move to the next level of faith and glory. In the passage below, Jesus is speaking to the Father and He testifies that He has released the same glory to us that the Father gave to Him. I find this to be very amazing and awesome.

> *And the glory which You gave Me I have given them, that they may be one just as We are one: I in them, and You in Me; that they may be made perfect in one, and that the world may know that You have sent Me, and have loved them as You have loved Me* (John 17:22-23).

Did you catch that? You can receive the same Glory that God gave to Jesus. Wow! That is an awesome thought! But, do you really believe that? Do you believe that you can carry the same glory that Jesus carried? Most believers do not truly believe this. If we don't believe what He said, how can we say that we believe in Jesus? In verse 23, we see the foundation for this statement. Jesus also testifies that Father God loves us just as He loves Jesus! That is so awesome!

There is something very special and very powerful in this prayer from Jesus in John, Chapter Seventeen. Notice: It is unity which opens the heavens. It is unity which prepares you to move in the anointing that the Lord is releasing to you. We have tried for too long to make it a solo experience. But, that is not in accordance with what Jesus said. In my book, "Seven Levels of Glory," I write about receiving a revelation directly from the Lord. He told me that "Unity Glory" is the highest level of glory we can experience on the earth. This is the level of glory we will live in when we are finally in heaven with Him for eternity. Why not begin now?

> *I do not pray for these alone, but also for those who will believe in Me through their word; that they all may be one, as You, Father, are in Me, and I in You; that they also may be one in Us, that the world may believe that You sent Me* (John 17:20-21).

It is Jesus' prayer that you have access to all that the disciples received. Do you think the Father answers Jesus' prayers? Notice the purpose for this -- it is unity glory! It is all about unity. That was Jesus' purpose! That was His mission! He called us to be at this level, but few have ever reached it and fewer still have been able to maintain it. Yet, this is the key to the anointing which the Lord is releasing.

Think about this: The disciples were arguing over who was the greatest in their group. They wanted to know who would be in charge after Jesus' departure, and who would sit on His right hand or left hand in the Kingdom. They thought this was their little secret, but He saw it all. Think about the depth of His anointing as a seer. Consider this verse from Luke 9:47 (ONMB), "*But since Y'shua saw the thoughts of their hearts,*" Jesus could see their inmost thoughts.

As I mentioned above, Jesus saw the Father and what the Father was doing! This was all part of God's plan for Jesus and for us through the work of Jesus. Jesus said that the Father showed Him all things! That is really deep. Can you imagine this for yourself? We need to go deeper in our understanding and in our relationship with the Lord. The Father showed Jesus greater and greater things, and

71

He will do the same for you! This anointing has a progressive nature. At a very high level in the seer anointing, Jesus could say, "*And He said to them, 'I saw Satan fall like lightning from heaven.'*" (Luke 10:18)

Recently, the Lord has been fulfilling a prophetic word given to me several weeks ago. Heaven has been coming down and opening up in the places where we are meeting. We see angels who seem to be on fire joining in worship with us. Angels start to manifest in the room. Many people see them and feel their presence. When this manifests, an anointing is present to impart a seer gifting to those present and many are receiving it. Others have their visions enhanced to the level of Ultra HD. I am sharing this because it is also available to you! I want you to reflect again on the passage below. Say it out loud over and over until you own it!

Most assuredly, I say to you, he who believes in Me, the works that I do he will do also; and greater works than these he will do, because I go to My Father (John 14:12).

These things are supposed to be manifesting in our ministry and in our meetings. We should experience the same things Jesus and the disciples experienced. We are to see more and more in the spiritual realm and do greater and greater things! Amen? Are you ready for it? The Lord spoke to me and said to elevate people to the level of "whatever." At first I didn't understand this so I asked for wisdom and revelation. He led me to the passage below. If you want to be elevated to the level of "whatever," speak it aloud over and over until you own it in your heart!

And whatever you ask in My name, that I will do, that the Father may be glorified in the Son. If you ask anything in My name, I will do it (John 14:13-14).

What should we expect when we go to the Lord in prayer? We should be absolutely confident that Jesus spoke the truth! We should believe that we will receive whatever we ask in His Name! I asked for wisdom to understand this, and the Lord told me that it was "whatever" we ask in accordance with who He is, within His will and His purposes, and for the glory of the Father!

A little while, and you will not see Me; and again a little while, and you will see Me, because I go to the Father (John 16:16).

According to this verse, we should be seeing the risen Lord! The Disciples saw Him! We should be seeing Him? Do you believe this? I think this is the core question. Do we truly believe what Jesus said? Do we truly believe in His promises? Are we ready to step out in faith and appropriate all the promises of the Lord in our lives and in our service? I am ready! How about you? Meditate again on the passage below. It is the key to our being enabled to walk in this level of anointing!

I do not pray for these alone, but also for those who will believe in Me through their word; that they all may be one, as You, Father, are in Me, and I in You; that they also may be one in Us, that the world may believe that You sent Me. And the glory which You gave Me I have given them, that they may be one just as We are one: I in them, and You in Me; that they may be made perfect in one, and that the world may know that You have sent Me, and have loved them as You have loved Me (John 17:20-23).

Believe and remember that all the things Jesus was releasing to the disciples are also for us! Do you believe this? Then it is time to take a faith challenge. Let's see what Jesus said. Then see if you really believe this is for you and your ministry. Don't forget to read it aloud over and over until it takes up residence in your heart.

Father, I desire that they also whom You gave Me may be with Me where I am, that they may behold My glory which You have given Me; for You loved Me before the foundation of the world (John 17:24).

Simply put, we should be seeing His glory! If we are born again, we should be seeing the kingdom (glory). Claim the promise of Jesus in Luke 9:27: "*But I tell you truly, there are some standing here who shall not taste death till they see the kingdom of God.*" Three of them saw Jesus transfigured in His glory. Nine of them missed it. Three of them saw Moses and Elijah. Nine of them missed it. Three of them saw the cloud of God's presence. Nine of them missed it. Three of them heard the voice of the Father, and nine of them missed it. I want to go against the odds and receive it all! How about you? Then you should be carrying His glory! Right? (See John 17:22) The Father loves you the same as He loves Jesus! Right? (See John 17:23) Remember that when you have seen Jesus, you have seen it all.

The Son is the radiance of God's glory and the exact representation of his being, sustaining all things by his powerful word. After he had provided purification

74

for sins, he sat down at the right hand of the Majesty in heaven (Hebrews 1:3).

SO WHAT IS BLOCKING SO MANY BELIEVERS?

I want to quickly go through a couple of the major roadblocks limiting many believers. These things seem self-evident. However, they need to be said over and over. The Lord certainly repeated them frequently in His Word. Many people who say they know this still allow it to block them. You cannot have it both ways. You must choose whether to hold on to the things which separate you from the Lord; or to let go and let God's full blessing come to you.

A. REBELLION WILL BLOCK YOUR GIFT!

Now the word of the Lord came to me, saying: "Son of man, you dwell in the midst of a rebellious house, which has eyes to see but does not see, and ears to hear but does not hear; for they are a rebellious house" (Ezekiel 12:1-2).

Ezekiel was clearly told by the Lord that he was dwelling in a rebellious house. You may be from another nation, but you are dwelling in a rebellious house. Every nation in the world is currently in rebellion against the Lord. This is most likely the main roadblock to the nations in the areas of prosperity and health. You simply cannot walk in the blessing and favor of God and be rebellious and disobedient. You must clear this up if you want to experience the Open Heaven. I have good news. The Lord has a plan to get you back into a right relationship with Him. Love and obey everything Jesus commanded and it will all work out for you!

B. DISOBEDIENCE WILL BLOCK YOUR GIFT

Now Moses called all Israel and said to them: "You have seen all that the Lord did before your eyes in the land of Egypt, to Pharaoh and to all his servants and to all his land—the great trials which your eyes have seen, the signs, and those great wonders. Yet the Lord has not given you a heart to perceive and eyes to see and ears to hear, to this very day" (Deuteronomy 29:1-4).

It is amazing to watch ourselves and others try to fool God. The scriptures warn us that God will not be mocked. He knows everything. He knows every act of disobedience in your life and work. The good news is that He loves you anyway and He has a plan to help you work it out. Once again the answer is to love and obey everything Jesus commanded. It isn't as difficult as it sounds. The Lord will actually help you do it. He has sent the Holy Spirit for this specific purpose. Now is the time to truly become a spirit-let believer.

ADDITIONAL SCRIPTURAL KEYS TO ASSIST YOU

KEEPING YOUR GIFT ACTIVE

Pursue love, and desire spiritual gifts, but especially that you may prophesy (1 Corinthians 14:1).

It's like the old joke about a man asking how he could get to Carnegie Hall. The answer he received was "practice, practice, practice." We keep our gifts active by using them. Spiritual gifts are like muscles. If you don't use them they atrophy. We keep strong and agile through exercising the body. The same is true for the spirit. It is time for a good spiritual workout. Use you gifts at every opportunity. Ask now for you seer anointing to open up and practice seeing spiritual things.

> *But solid food belongs to those who are of full age, that is, those who by reason of use have their senses exercised to discern both good and evil (Hebrews 5:14).*

USE EACH GIFT FOR ITS PROPER PURPOSE!

> *But he who prophesies speaks edification and exhortation and comfort to men (1 Corinthians 14:3).*

I have witnessed so many poor uses of the prophetic or seer gifts. I have seen people use them to gain power and influence. I have seen people trying to use them for their own personal gain. I have seen people using their gifts to attempt to control other people. When the spirit of control is used it is most often the Jezebel spirit. You must avoid this at all costs. Break off the spirit of control and set your spirit free in Yeshua's Name! Plead the blood of Jesus over yourself so this spirit cannot return! Amen!

We need to line up with the teachings of the Word. The Lord wants us to bless others and not to curse them. He wants us to help them reach a desired outcome rather than to be cast down in judgment and condemnation. May our prophetic words release edification, exhortation and comfort to the Lord's people! I also like the way it is said in the NIV:

> *But everyone who prophesies speaks to men for their strengthening, encouragement and comfort (1 Corinthians 14:3, NIV).*

BE ZEALOUS FOR YOUR ANOINTING AND GIFTS!

Even so you, since you are zealous for spiritual gifts, let it be for the edification of the church that you seek to excel (1 Corinthians 14:12).

Paul expands on the idea of helping to edify individuals. This gift is also for the entire body of Christ. May you use your spiritual gifts to build up the church! May you use your gifts to strengthen the Body in order to reach the world for Christ! May your gifts always be used for the Lord's purposes! May they bring comfort to those in your ministry! Amen!

If you don't know what to do with a prophetic word which reveals a character defect or a personal sin, then ask the Lord to give you a "word of wisdom." When we let the Spirit lead us, He will tells us how, when and where to do it. He will also tell us how to help them achieve the Lord's desired outcome for their lives and ministries. Our calling is to build them up and not to tear them down!

WIN UNBELIEVERS

But if all prophesy, and an unbeliever or an uninformed person comes in, he is convinced by all, he is convicted by all. And thus the secrets of his heart are revealed; and so, falling down on his face, he will worship God and report that God is truly among you (1 Corinthians 14:24-25).

It seems obvious from Paul's teaching that the Lord wants all of us to have the gift of prophesy! This is also obvious from the prophecy of Joel and in Peter's sermon on the Day of Pentecost. It is great to earnestly desire the gifts, but it is better to desire them for their intended purpose: to win the lost. You may all prophesy! Always remember what comes first. You are to pursue the love of God so that you can release His words with His love.

For you can all prophesy one by one, that all may learn and all may be encouraged (1 Corinthians 14:31).

It is time to take control of your own spirit! I remind you again of Paul's words in 1 Corinthians 14:32, *"And the spirits of the prophets are subject to the prophets."* You must continually seek to activate and increase your seer anointing! Take to heart what Paul said in 1 Corinthians 14:39-40, *"Therefore, brethren, desire earnestly to prophesy, and do not forbid to speak with tongues. Let all things be done decently and in order."* It is good to desire these gifts. It is also good to help others exercise their gifts.

There are things the lord wants to show you right now! There are things He wants to release for the whole body, but His plan is to tell us first. Consider what the Lord said in Amos 3:7, *"Surely the Lord GOD does nothing, unless He reveals His secret to His servants the prophets."* When we are truly ready to follow His plan He will release it to us. He will even do more than that. He will continue to show us greater things and release us to do them!

IMPARTATION

I believe this can be imparted because it is in the Word and it is within the Will of the Father. You don't have to have someone else do this for you. You can do it! Right now, touch your eyes and command them to see! Then touch your ears and command them to hear! You may need to do this over and over! Always press in for more.

How about releasing Ultra HD visions to your spiritual eyes! Speak it over your spirit and let the Holy Spirit do the rest! Amen and Amen!!!!

PRAYER

For this reason we also, since the day we heard it, do not cease to pray for you, and to ask that you may be filled with the knowledge of His will in all wisdom and spiritual understanding; that you may walk worthy of the Lord, fully pleasing Him, being fruitful in every good work and increasing in the knowledge of God; strengthened with all might, according to His glorious power, for all patience and longsuffering with joy; giving thanks to the Father who has qualified us to be partakers of the inheritance of the saints in the light. He has delivered us from the power of darkness and conveyed us into the kingdom of the Son of His love, in whom we have redemption through His blood, the forgiveness of sins. He is the image of the invisible God, the firstborn over all creation. For by Him all things were created that are in heaven and that are on earth, visible and invisible, whether thrones or dominions or principalities or powers. All things were created through Him and for Him. And He is before all things, and in Him all things consist. And He is the head of the body, the church, who is the beginning, the firstborn from the dead, that in all things He may have the preeminence (Colossians 1:9-18).

PAUSE AND REFLECT

1. In what ways is your spirit subject to you?

2. How can you awaken your seer anointing?

3. Why is it important for you to awaken this anointing?

4. What can you do to receive these kingdom keys?

5. In what ways has the Lord revealed the open heavens to you?

6. How does the fear of the Lord help you see an open heaven?

7. In the space below write decrees to open the heavens for you?

8. What does Jesus want you to see?

9. Why is it important to read the Word of God aloud?

CHAPTER 4

LOVE OPENS HEAVEN

Key 4: LOVE

Now Moses called all Israel and said to them: "You have seen all that the Lord did before your eyes in the land of Egypt, to Pharaoh and to all his servants and to all his land—the great trials which your eyes have seen, the signs, and those great wonders. Yet the Lord has not given you a heart to perceive and eyes to see and ears to hear, to this very day" (Deuteronomy 29:2-4).

This passage captured my thoughts and raised some questions in my mind. Has the Lord given us a "heart to perceive?" Most of us have seen the signs and wonders. We have witnessed great healing miracles. That is a good thing, but has the Lord given us a "heart to perceive?" What do all the signs and wonders mean if we haven't received a heart to perceive them? Are we in the same situation as the Hebrews when Moses spoke to them? Do we lack the eyes which can see and understand the things of the Spirit? Do we lack the ears to hear what the Lord is saying and understand it? I pray that we will receive what the Lord has freely given through the finished work of Jesus Christ! Amen?

I want to share something deeply personal with you. I am praying that the Lord will give you a heart to perceive, eyes to see and ears to hear. The problem I experienced in the past was trying to see spiritual things through my natural senses. The Lord is working now to awaken our spiritual heart, eyes, and ears. I pray that you and I will not resist Him as they did! Amen? This is what the Lord did to me! This is what the Lord did for me! It was not any type of work of my own. It was strictly a gift from the Lord:

The pastor and I entered the church several minutes after the worship had begun. I was led to two seats where we would wait for my time to give a message to the congregation. Suddenly something amazing happened to me. I was completely unprepared for this to happen. It felt like the air in the room suddenly took on great weight and all of it came down and rested on me. It was so heavy that I was completely unable to move. I could not turn my head, move my body or even wiggly my fingers. I was literally pinned to the chair unable to move. My mind was racing. I thought about the ministry time which was rapidly approaching. I didn't have any idea how I was going to stand up and speak to this group of people. I couldn't move a muscle because of the heavy weight which had settled down on me. A little bit of panic began to set in. What if I was introduced and just sat there motionless? What if the weight didn't lift? How long could I just sit there motionless in the church? This was a very awkward moment for me.

After what seemed like a very long time, my head loosened slightly and I was able to turn my head very slowly toward my left. Then I began to get a look at the people who had gathered in the church. At this point, I began to have a strange feeling. I felt so much love for the people.

The love I felt was amazing and so powerful. I had never felt like this before. At first it was a wonderful feeling, but it soon became problematic. The first few people who came into view were all women, and I felt this amazing love for them. It was almost like falling in love. This seemed very inappropriate, and I prayed for help from the Lord. Then I heard His voice. He said, "That is not your love! It is my love for the people!" I was in awe of the Fathers love. I suddenly realized that I had known very little about His love in the past. I had known about it with my mind, but I had not been overwhelmed by it in my spirit the way I experienced at that moment.

As I continued to visually pan across the room, I noticed that I had this same feeling of love for the men and children. The feeling in my heart was exactly like I had experienced for the women I had seen right after this anointing came over me. I realized that I was seeing people differently. I was seeing them as the Lord sees them with His eyes of love. I knew that I was only experiencing that love in part because of my human limitations. Yet, it was so overpoweringly strong. I began to understand how much the Lord loves us, and I wanted to communicate this to others. I quickly learned that I do not have the ability to release what I was feeling to others in words. I desperately wanted people to know the depth of the Father's love for them. I realized that until now I had never fully understood what Paul was talking about in Ephesians, Chapter Three:

For this reason I bow my knees to the Father of our Lord Jesus Christ, from whom the whole family in heaven and earth is named, that He would grant you, according to the riches of His glory, to be strengthened with might through His Spirit in the inner man, that Christ may dwell in your hearts through faith;

that you, being rooted and grounded in love, may be able to comprehend with all the saints what is the width and length and depth and height—to know the love of Christ which passes knowledge; that you may be filled with all the fullness of God (Ephesians 3:14-19).

Later that day, during the ministry time, I was imparting the Father's love into the hands of all the people and giving many of them prophetic words. As I looked down at their hands, I saw something amazing. Many of the hands were not pretty by human standards. Some of the people worked outdoors and their hands looked like they were made of leather. Some were twisted and damaged from years of hard labor. As I looked at those hands I saw them from the Lord's perspective. He absolutely loves the hands of those who labor in righteousness. I wanted to honor the hands of each person and just touch them with the Father's love.

At that moment, my deepest heart's desire was to tell them how much the Father loves them. This desire hasn't changed since that experience. I just want to somehow be enabled to tell people *"what is the width and length and depth and height"* of the love of Christ. I want them to know how this love allows them to *"be filled with all the fullness of God."* I want them to experience the power of His love to shatter every self-doubt. I want them to be set free from their poor self-image. I want the love of the Father to give them such a powerful breakthrough that all the lies of the enemy will just fall away and set them free.

Every time I stand up to minister to the Lord's people, this love comes back. I often just stop and look into the faces of those beloved by the Lord. As I do this, I get filled again with that awe and amazement. Each time this happens, I am filled with a desire to share the Love of God with His beloved children. Over and over, I experience my inadequacy to communicate the fullness of this love to people. Yet, I can't help myself. The Love of the Father compels me to continue to reach out to His people and release His love for them.

My prayer is that others will experience this same weighty presence of the Father's love. My prayer is that you will be so filled with that love that it will totally transform all your relationships. I want to share it with you and others and inspire you to spread this wonderful news of the Father's love. I pray for you, the reader, to just wait on the Lord and allow this heavy blanket of His Glory to rest on you! Let Him fill you to overflowing with all His fullness of love and grace! Amen and Amen!!!

THE FOURTH KEY TO OPEN HEAVEN

THE KEY OF LOVE

Love is actually the second most powerful key given to us so that we can open heaven. The first of course is Yeshua. I chose to list it as the fourth key because you need the other keys to grasp this one. You need Yeshua and His powerful message that the Kingdom of Heaven is at hand. You definitely need to know that the kingdom of God is at hand and you can press into it. You need for your spiritual eyes to be opened wide in order to see and experience it. When you receive these things, you are better prepared to experience this extreme love for others. Remember: I am not talking about human love which tends to come and go. I am talking about something much greater and truly beyond all human understanding. This very powerful Key to open Heaven is from beginning to end based solely on the FATHER'S LOVE!

Human love is always inadequate for the task. Jesus knew that. This is why he said, *"But I know you, that you do not have the love of God in you."* (John 5:42) Since it is not in us, we cannot generate it out of our own hearts. We need to have God's love imparted to us and infused into us. The good news is that God is faithful and good and is still willing to provide His love to people like you and me. Read aloud, over and over, the passages below and let this understanding fill your heart and your mind with the knowledge of this great mystery.

- *Now hope does not disappoint, because the love of God has been poured out in our hearts by the Holy Spirit who was given to us* (Romans 5:5).

- *Now may the Lord direct your hearts into the love of God and into the patience of Christ* (2 Thessalonians 3:5).

- *But whoever keeps His word, truly the love of God is perfected in him. By this we know that we are in Him* (1 John 2:5).

- But *whoever has this world's goods, and sees his brother in need, and shuts up his heart from him, how does the love of God abide in him* (1 John 3:17)?

- *But you, beloved, building yourselves up on your most holy faith, praying in the Holy Spirit, keep yourselves in the love of God, looking for the mercy of our Lord Jesus Christ unto eternal life* (Jude 1:20-21).

All these passages have one thing in common. They are speaking of God's love and not about our love for Him. They are speaking about a kind of love which has to be "spilled out in our hearts." He doesn't just plant a little seed and wait for it to grow in the fertile soil of our hearts. It doesn't work like that, and we are not able to do our part of the process. Our behavior will show others whether we have it or not. You cannot fake the love of God. It is genuine, pure, holy and life giving. There are no counterfeits for the love of God. You must have the original and genuine thing if you are going to be fully equipped for His ministry. There is only one source and the only way to get it is through the work of the Holy Spirit. I constantly pray for more! I want a greater anointing and a greater infilling of His love! How about you?

I believe that the Lord is the same yesterday, today, and forever. What He released to His people in the past, He is willing and able to release to His people today. What He has released to me, He will impart to you! As the seed of the Word of God begins to grow in your heart, let your spirit fully embrace the awesome love of the Father, the love of Jesus Christ and the love of the Holy Spirit for you and all those around you. Once you begin to experience more and more of the depth of His love, make a covenant to never let it go. Always endeavor to keep yourself in the love of God and keep the Love of God in your heart!

Beloved, let us love one another, for love is of God; and everyone who loves is born of God and knows God. He who does not love does not know God, for God is love. In this the love of God was manifested toward us, that God has sent His only begotten Son into the world, that we might live through Him. In this is love, not that we loved God, but that He loved us and sent His Son to be the propitiation for our sins. Beloved, if God so loved us, we also ought to love one another (1 John 4:7-11).

ABIDING IN LOVE IS THE KEY TO ABIDING IN GOD

And we have known and believed the love that God has for us. God is love, and he who abides in love abides in God, and God in him (1 John 4:16).

Remember that it is all about Him. It is not that we first loved Him. He is the one who initiates it and brings it to completion. We are told over and over to draw near to Him and He will draw near to us. Too many people are waiting until they feel good enough to receive it. That time will never come. You cannot be good enough to abide with Him and in His love; but there is good news. He has taken care of the problem for you. He sent Jesus and then covered you with His robe of righteousness. He cleansed you with Yeshua's blood. It is from first to last a work of God in Yeshua ha Messiach! All you have to do is receive it. Are you ready to receive it now?

ABIDING IN LOVE IS THE KEY TO INTIMACY WITH THE LORD

Jesus answered and said to him, "If anyone loves Me, he will keep My word; and My Father will love him, and We will come to him and make Our home with him. He who does not love Me does not keep My words; and the word which you hear is not Mine but the Father's who sent Me" (John 14:23-24).

It appears that the process is supposed to begin with us learning to love Jesus. This really isn't as easy as it sounds. We keep making the same mistake. We believe that somehow we can develop that love in our own hearts and elevate it to a level which pleases the Lord. But I want to assure you of one thing. You just cannot do it.

The result for many people who try to do it on their own is that they get frustrated with their failures to produce this love. Then they want to give up. This is not God's way for us. He is the source of this love. It is impossible for you to produce it on your own. So, quit being frustrated! Stop feeling like a failure. Learn the most important lesson of love. Go to the Father and let Him fill you with His love. It is the only way to make it work. The good news is that this is exactly what the Father wants to do for you.

LOVE BINDS US TOGETHER

Love is the key to building a relationship with the Lord. It is also the key to building relationships with one another. Love truly opens the kingdom of God in our hearts and allows the Lord to dwell with us and in us. Love is the beginning and end of our relationship with Him as His disciples. Love is like the super glue of the spiritual realm. Only the love of God can raise us up to the Unity Level of Glory. Unity is the end product of the Father's love and it is the goal of Jesus' ministry. Therefore, it should be the ultimate goal of our ministry.

Jesus replied, "If anyone loves me, he will obey my teaching. My Father will love him, and we will come to him and make our home with him" (John 14:23).

TO DEAL WITH THE ENEMY

YOU NEED THE WHOLE ARMOR OF GOD!

There is an old holistic health saying which goes something like this, "If the only tool you have is a hammer, everything looks like a nail." I am sharing this to say that we must be careful about how we use the armor of God.

There is a temptation to put on the armor to deal with each other. There is a temptation to protect ourselves from harm by getting behind protective walls. We need the love of God to draw us out again. There is a temptation to use our spiritual weapons against each other when we feel threatened. But, we must never forget that our battle is not with flesh and blood.

> *Finally, my brethren, be strong in the Lord and in the power of His might. Put on the whole armor of God, that you may be able to stand against the wiles of the devil. For we do not wrestle against flesh and blood, but against principalities, against powers, against the rulers of the darkness of this age, against spiritual hosts of wickedness in the heavenly places. Therefore take up the whole armor of God, that you may be able to withstand in the evil day, and having done all, to stand* (Ephesians 6:10-13).

Many people live with their protective armor on all the time. They wear it as a protection in almost all of their relationships with others. Many people who live this way have been hurt deeply by others in the past. Now, they are trying desperately to avoid being hurt again. Tragically, this behavior which was designed to protect them actually results in more hurts. People who do this often find themselves standing alone. People who constantly wear their armor soon become isolated and alone. This is not the Father's heart for us. He wants to draw us out and draw us together with His love.

We need a different kind of clothing to deal with one another. The good news is that the Lord has already provided all we need. As you study the Word of God, you will find that there are many different kinds of apparel for those who are in Christ Jesus. In His first recorded sermon,

Jesus releases a powerful picture of His anointing which was first proclaimed by the prophet Isaiah hundreds of years earlier. A major part of Yeshua's mission was to get us properly clothed for Kingdom business. Yeshua is the source of our proper attire for this life and the next.

> *The Spirit of the Lord GOD is upon Me, because the Lord has anointed Me to preach good tidings to the poor; He has sent Me to heal the brokenhearted, to proclaim liberty to the captives, and the opening of the prison to those who are bound; to proclaim the acceptable year of the Lord, and the day of vengeance of our God; to comfort all who mourn, to console those who mourn in Zion, to give them beauty for ashes, the oil of joy for mourning, the gar-ment of praise for the spirit of heaviness; That they may be called trees of righteousness, the planting of the Lord, that He may be glorified* (Isaiah 61:1-3).

Jesus gives a garment of praise in place of a spirit of heaviness. We need to suit up every day with this garment to cover and protect us from the wiles of the devil. Too many people seem more comfortable with a spirit of heaviness than with this amazing and wonderful garment of praise. They have experienced so much hurt that they are unable to summon up any words or even thoughts of praise. Tragically, they are blocking the solution to their own situation. Praise breaks the power of the enemy and protects us from every demonic spirit.

If this was the only garment the Lord gives, it would be sufficient. But, the Lord has even better news for us. He has many more garments for us. He has a garment for every spiritual need we may have. The Lord is saying, "I've got you covered! Whatever the challenge may be, you can trust me! I've truly got you covered!" Are you wearing your coverings to give you all the protection you need to deal with the strategies and attacks by the enemy? The Lord wants to give you more! Are you ready for it? Isaiah describes more of these new spiritual garments.

I delight greatly in the LORD; my soul rejoices in my God. For he has clothed me with garments of salvation and arrayed me in a robe of his righteousness, as a bridegroom adorns his head like a priest, and as a bride adorns herself with her jewels (Isaiah 61:10, NIV).

This is such a powerful description of what the Lord won for us on that terrible and torturous cross. He wants to provide you with "*garments of salvation.*" I believe that this is released in the plural because the Lord's salvation is for spirit, soul, and body. He saves us from sin and death. He saves us from oppression and despair. He saves us from attacks by our enemies in both the natural and spiritual realms. He saves us from all judgment and condemnation. Hallelujah! Thank you Lord for providing these amazing and wonderful garments of salvation! Thank you for the price you paid!

The Lord also provides us with a robe of his righteousness. It is so important to catch this. It is his righteousness. He is so gracious to give us this wonderful covering. I love the way Isaiah says it: the Lord "arrayed me in a robe of His righteousness." You have been "arrayed" in the same way. I believe this robe has the very fragrance of Christ in it. This is what Paul meant when he wrote about the fragrance of Christ to the church at Corinth:

Now thanks be to God who always leads us in triumph in Christ, and through us diffuses the fragrance of His knowledge in every place. For we are to God the fragrance of Christ among those who are being saved and among those who are perishing (2 Corinthians 2:14-15).

This is not the end of the Lord's good news about how we are to be clothed as disciples of Jesus Christ. There is more and this relates directly to the topic of love. So, I want to tell you about another style of clothing. These are the garments of the Father's love. This love and these garments are being shed abroad in the hearts of His faithful followers.

Therefore, as God's chosen people, holy and dearly loved, clothe yourselves with compassion, kindness, humility, gentleness and patience. Bear with each other and forgive whatever grievances you may have against one another. Forgive as the Lord forgave you. And over all these virtues put on love, which binds them all together in perfect unity (Colossians 3:12-14).

Notice that it is our task to clothe ourselves in this manner. All of these character traits come as gifts from the Lord. Yet, we are told to take authority and put them on ourselves. Remember: "The spirits of the prophets are subject to the prophets." So, now it is time to put on: compassion, kindness, humility, gentleness and patience. We are to wear them as an outer garment when we minister and serve with others. These are the things the Lord wants people to see in us. He does this so that He can reach other people with the gospel and bring them into the kingdom of the Son of His love. We are to bear each other's burdens and forgive every offense. Rather than constantly being on the defensive, bear with each other. Forgive and forget! Then we can put on the best garment of all. We can wear the garment of His love! Wow! What a beautiful description of our calling in Christ Jesus!

But the end of all things is at hand; therefore be serious and watchful in your prayers. And above all things have fervent love for one another, for love will cover a multitude of sins (1 Peter 4:7-8).

The Lord does not give us bland and tired old garments to wear in self-debasing humility. He gives us intense, colorful, and powerful garments so that we can do what He does and say what He says with our appearance as well as well as with our words. His garments have brilliant and vivid colors which proclaim the awesome wonder of His love. We are to have *"fervent love for one another."* When we are enabled to carry the Father's love like Jesus did, we will experience a new level of anointing. Peter says that this *"love will cover a multitude of sins."*

I believe that this kind of love is like a double edge sword. It cuts both ways. On the one hand, it enables us to cover over the sins of others so that we can see them and love them like the Father. On the other hand, this love will cover over the sin in our own lives to set us free to do what the Lord is calling us to do! This is the love which will bind us together. It lifts us up to the unity level of glory where we can experience the fullness of God.

The most powerful tool the devil uses against us is tempting us to be offended with each other. It is like bait on a fisherman's hook. When we bite the bait, the enemy sinks the hook deeply into our souls. He takes control and authority over things which were never meant for him. The truth is that when we live with offense, we have already lost the battle. We need to take back the authority the Lord has given us (Luke 10:19) and reclaim the power and control over our own lives which the Lord won for us at such great cost.

Paul says it this way in Galatians 5:15, *"If you bite and devour each other, watch out or you will be destroyed by each other.*" Instead of building each other up, we are tearing each other down. This is not the way of the Lord. By this kind of behavior, we lose our witness to the world. Our greatest witness is our love for one another. This love is above and beyond all that the world has to offer. When people see this love, they will know that it is from God the Father, and they will be drawn to Him. Read Jesus' command again and really take it to heart. We must love others as He loved us. We cannot do that with human love. We are going to have to have an outpouring of the Father's love. Then the world will take note and believe we are truly His disciples.

A new command I give you: Love one another. As I have loved you, so you must love one another. By this everyone will know that you are my disciples, if you love one another (John 13:34-35).

AS OFFENSE SEPARATES US

LOVE BINDS US TOGETHER

Our greatest strength is revealed when we are bound together in unity. Remember that unity elevates us to the level of "whatever." Remember what Jesus said in Matthew 18:19, "*Again I say to you that if two of you agree on earth concerning anything that they ask, it will be done for them by My Father in heaven.*" Why did Jesus say it again? We need to hear it over and over. We need to speak it with our own mouths. We are called to release the full power of this promise to others. Remember: You can only give away what you have received.

Always remember that your greatest tool in ministry as well as in spiritual warfare is love. This is so much more powerful than all of the enemy's tools. You can overcome every spiritual challenge with the love of the Father shed abroad in your heart. In the same way, our greatest witness to the world is loving one another. Paul said it this way in Romans 5:5 (KJV), "*And hope maketh not ashamed; because the love of God is shed abroad in our hearts by the Holy Ghost which is given unto us.*"

The disciples of Jesus Christ needed both the power of unity and the power of speech to share the gospel on the Day of Pentecost. This is one of the most dramatic illustrations of what we are talking about in this chapter of the book. When the fire of God came, it seemed to weld them together more than ever before. They became one in spirit and in truth. They stood together in unity for the first time. They became empowered and emboldened by the love of God.

When the Day of Pentecost had fully come, they were all with one accord in one place. And suddenly there came a sound from heaven, as of a rushing mighty wind, and it filled the whole house where they were sitting. Then there appeared to them divided tongues, as of fire, and one sat upon each of them. And they were all filled with the Holy Spirit and began to speak with other tongues, as the Spirit gave them utterance (Acts 2:1-4).

This was really the first time they were all in one accord. The power of God didn't lead to pride and disunity. It joined them in wonderful ways. It was more powerful than anything they had experienced before. Common men without formal education were speaking fluently in a number of different languages. Or did they speak one language and everyone present was enabled by the Holy Spirit to understand their message? Either way, it speaks of a whole new level of unity which had been released to the Body of Christ. They were now moving in unity with one another and in sync with the Holy Spirit. The result was amazing. Thousands were drawn to the Lord by the witness of their unity and love. This is what the Lord is calling us to do today!

THE HOLY SPIRIT BROUGHT

A NEW LEVEL OF DISCERNMENT

Then Peter stood up with the Eleven, raised his voice and addressed the crowd: "Fellow Jews and all of you who live in Jerusalem, let me explain this to you; listen carefully to what I say. These people are not drunk, as you suppose. It's only nine in the morning! No, this is what was spoken by the prophet Joel: 'In the last days, God says, I will pour out my Spirit on all people. Your sons and daughters will prophesy, your young men will see visions, your old men will dream dreams. Even on my servants, both men and women, I will pour out my Spirit in those days, and they will prophesy. I will show wonders in the heavens above and signs on the earth below, blood and fire and billows of smoke. The sun will be turned to darkness and the moon to blood before the coming of the great and glorious day of the Lord. And everyone who calls on the name of the Lord will be saved'" (Acts 2:14-21).

What people saw and what Peter described in this speech seem very different on the surface. But there is much more to this story. People had seen the sun turned to darkness as Jesus hung on the cross. That night there was a blood moon which came as an announcement from the Lord that a new season had begun. They had seen the blood of Jesus! And now the fire of God had been released to the men and women who had gathered in the upper room. Everything prophesied by Joel had manifested, at least in part. It had not yet fallen on all flesh, but it was spreading quickly.

The good news for you and me is that this was only the beginning. God's plan extended far beyond what they could see that day. The people didn't see the complete and final fulfillment of Joel prophecy. They saw much of the fulfillment of the prophecy, but we are still waiting for the final chapter to be written. Just as the Holy Spirit gave Peter discernment into the meaning of Pentecost that day, He is still releasing more and more revelation for believers today. The Holy Spirit is now working out the fulfillment of Jesus promise:

However, when He, the Spirit of truth, has come, He will guide you into all truth; for He will not speak on His own authority, but whatever He hears He will speak; and He will tell you things to come. He will glorify Me, for He will take of what is Mine and declare it to you. All things that the Father has are Mine. Therefore I said that He will take of Mine and declare it to you (John 16:13-15).

WE ARE STILL WAITING FOR THE FULFILLMENT OF THIS PROPHECY

Little children, it is the last hour; and as you have heard that the Antichrist is coming, even now many antichrists have come, by which we know that it is the last hour. They went out from us, but they were not of us; for if they had been of us, they would have continued with us; but they went out that they might be made manifest, that none of them were of us. But you have an anointing from the Holy One, and you know all things. I have not written to you because you do not know the truth, but because you know it, and that no lie is of the truth (1 John 2:18-21).

Time is short and today more than ever, we need to stand in one accord. As John said we are in the last hour. The Day of the Lord is at hand and there is very little time to bring in the harvest of the Kingdom. If we are going to succeed in our God-given mission, we need to be in unity and be ready for his return. We need to put aside petty differences and be united in heart and purpose.

ONLY LOVE CAN BIND US TOGETHER IN THIS LAST HOUR

We have seen from the scriptures above that the love of God enables us to rise above petty difference and to overlook and overcome all offenses. We have seen that love covers a multitude of sins – ours and other's. This is the power of God at work in us to will and to do what He has anointed us to accomplish. Love unites us with the Lord and with one another. Love is powerful and it is like a garment to be worn by everyone who believes in the Lord, Jesus Christ.

In 1782, Pastor John Fawcett, left a small church in Wainsgate, England for a larger one in London. He wrote these words which are now in the public domain as a farewell message to the people he had loved and served for a long time. They are as powerful today as when he first penned them. Even if you are familiar with them, read them as if for the first time. Feel the love of God which binds our hearts!

"Blest be the tie that binds
Our hearts in Christian love;
The fellowship of kindred minds
Is like to that above.

We share each other's woes,
Our mutual burdens bear;
And often for each other flows
The sympathizing tear.

From sorrow, toil and pain,
And sin, we shall be free,
And perfect love and friendship reign
Through all eternity."

I close this chapter with one final reminder from Proverbs 27:17, *"As iron sharpens iron, so one man sharpens another."* Together in love and unity, we sharpened the skills, abilities, and witness of one another. In unity and in agreement, we release the power of God's love to transform a dark and dying world into the kingdom of the Son of His love. Read again the powerful prayer the Apostle Paul prayed over the Colossian Church. Let it become your prayer for yourself. Then begin to pray it over others. Pray it over your family, your friends and the members of your church.

For this reason we also, since the day we heard it, do not cease to pray for you, and to ask that you may be filled with the knowledge of His will in all wisdom and spiritual understanding; that you may walk worthy of the Lord, fully pleasing Him, being fruitful in every good work and increasing in the knowledge of God; strengthened with all might, according to His glorious power, for all patience and longsuffering with joy; giving thanks to the Father who has qualified us to be partakers of the inheritance of the saints in the light. He has delivered us from the power of darkness and conveyed us into the kingdom of the Son of His love, in whom we have redemption through His blood, the forgiveness of sins (Colossians 1:9-14).

PRAYER OF IMPARTATION FOR THE FATHER'S LOVE AND AN OPEN HEAVEN

For this reason I bow my knees to the Father of our Lord Jesus Christ, from whom the whole family in heaven and earth is named, that He would grant you, according to the riches of His glory, to be strengthened with might through His Spirit in the inner man, that Christ may dwell in your hearts through faith; that you, being rooted and grounded in love, may be able to comprehend with all the saints what is the width and length and depth and height—to know the love of Christ which passes knowledge; that you may be filled with all the fullness of God. Now to Him who is able to do exceedingly abundantly above all that we ask or think, according to the power that works in us, to Him be glory in the church by Christ Jesus to all generations, forever and ever. Amen (Ephesians 3:14-21).

PAUSE AND REFLECT

1. List some of the ways the Love of God has been poured into your heart.

2. How do you learn to love more?

3. How is love the key to obedience (John 14:23)?

4. When is it inappropriate to wear your armor and use your spiritual weapons?

5. Which garments have you received from the Lord?

6. How has the love of God changed your life and ministry?

CHAPTER 5

OBEDIENCE OPENS HEAVEN

Key 5: OBEDIENCE

I want to share with you another key to the Open Heaven. When I have taught this in the past, I always ask people, "Does that sound okay?" They usually answer, "Yes!" Then I say to them, "Perhaps you will not like it. But, it is the truth! Do you want to know the truth?" The reason I do this is because I have found that people don't really like to talk about or hear about obedience. But if you want to live under an Open Heaven, you've got to deal with this key. Remember what Jesus said about the truth! Knowing the truth will set you free.

> *To the Jews who had believed him, Jesus said, "f you hold to my teaching, you are really my disciples. Then you will know the truth, and the truth will set you free"* (John 8:31-32).

It seems like people are born with a rebellious spirit. From an early age they choose to be disobedient and have their own way. It is a challenge to teach children of any age to obey. This has always been a sticking point in the church. Many churches have chosen to ignore the topic in order to be more "seeker friendly." They are willing at times to compromise the truth in order to have larger numbers of people as members and participants in their programs. They want to make the way easy for people. However, I am convinced that we need to remember and follow what Jesus said about this.

> *Enter by the narrow gate; for wide is the gate and broad is the way that leads to destruction, and there are many who go in by it. Because narrow is the gate and difficult is the way which leads to life, and there are few who find it* (Matthew 7:13-14).

The truth is that there is a price to pay for disobedience. People need to know this in order to properly connect with the Lord. Conversely, there are numerous benefits and blessings for those who are obedient. We have to choose and we need to choose wisely. This is not a new teaching. The basic principles were laid out by Moses long ago. Study and meditate on the blessings mentioned in the passage below.

> *If you fully obey the Lord your God and carefully follow all his commands I give you today, the Lord your God will set you high above all the nations on earth. All these blessings will come upon you and accompany you if you obey the Lord your God: You will be blessed in the city and blessed in the country. The fruit of your womb will be blessed, and the crops of your land and the young of your live-stock—the calves of your herds and the lambs of your flocks. Your basket and your kneading trough will be blessed. You will be blessed when you come in and blessed when you go out. The Lord will grant*

that the enemies who rise up against you will be defeated before you. They will come at you from one direction but flee from you in seven. The Lord will send a blessing on your barns and on everything you put your hand to. The Lord your God will bless you in the land he is giving you. The Lord will establish you as his holy people, as he promised you on oath, if you keep the commands of the Lord your God and walk in his ways. Then all the peoples on earth will see that you are called by the name of the Lord, and they will fear you. The Lord will grant you abundant prosperity—in the fruit of your womb, the young of your livestock and the crops of your ground—in the land he swore to your forefathers to give you. The Lord will open the heavens, the storehouse of his bounty, to send rain on your land in season and to bless all the work of your hands. You will lend to many nations but will borrow from none. The Lord will make you the head, not the tail. If you pay attention to the commands of the Lord your God that I give you this day and carefully follow them, you will always be at the top, never at the bottom. Do not turn aside from any of the commands I give you today, to the right or to the left, following other gods and serving them (Deuteronomy 28:1-14).

When the Lord first began lifting me up to Heaven on a regular basis, He told me to write a book and explain to people why they were being invited to make these kinds of visits to the third Heaven. Over a period of several weeks, the Lord taught me the contents of the book, "*Beyond the Ancient Door – Free to Move About the Heavens*." During one of these visits, I asked the Lord why some people were not able to experience these things, and His answer was, "My Grace!" He went on to explain that people who were told in Heaven what He wanted them to do and then refused to do it would quickly come under judgment. He explained that this is a season of grace and He doesn't want to bring judgment to people at this time. So, He is waiting until they are ready to obey before bringing them up into His presence.

Then the Lord told me that He was going to use me as an example. I was not thrilled to hear this. Being an example is often a painful process. The Lord then told me to do four things; to move to another city; write the book; tell people about my visits to Heaven; and release impartation for third Heaven visitation. I did not want to do any of these things. I immediately understood the price I would have to pay to obey the commands of the Lord. I saw it clearly and knew it would not be easy. However, it was also painfully clear that I would experience judgment quickly if I refused to do as the Lord commanded. So, I chose to obey. Just as I suspected, it was not easy and there was a big price to pay. I started to lose friends and associates right away. I became the object of anger, judgment, ridicule and condemnation by many people.

What I did not see at that time was what the Lord would give to me in place of all the things I would lose. He is so good and He has blessed me in so many ways. I have new friends who stand by me. I have a new area of ministry where I can freely do as the Lord asks. I have been set free from the fear of man and released to fear the Lord in the beauty of His holiness. I am so glad that I chose to obey. At first, all I could see was the price, but now I can see even more clearly the benefits of serving Him. I can say with all my heart today:

Bless the Lord, O my soul; and all that is within me, bless His holy name! Bless the Lord, O my soul, and forget not all His benefits: Who forgives all your iniquities, Who heals all your diseases, Who redeems your life from destruction, Who crowns you with lovingkindness and tender mercies, Who satisfies your mouth with good things, so that your youth is renewed like the eagle's (Psalm 103:1-5).

THE THIRD KEY IS OBEDIENCE

Remember how the Lord told me that many people do not experience the open Heaven because they are not ready to obey. I quickly found that many of these people actually think they are obedient. Their spiritual eyes have been blinded to the truth of their own spiritual condition. You probably know people who simply cannot admit any mistake or failure. They never truly experience their own forgiveness because they have not been willing to see their sin and repent. So, the Lord cannot release His amazing and wonderful forgiveness to them. This is very tragic!

Some other people tend to think of obedience in terms of the things they don't do. They can give you a list of all the things they have never done or that they have stopped doing. They see this list of "don't" as the fullness of obedience to the Lord. They think they are ready and obedient, but they don't fully understand the magnitude of God's plan. He is more concerned about what we do than what we do not do. Ask yourself about how obedient you are to the Lord's commands. See if you are measuring your obedience by the things you don't do. Hopefully, you have already caught the Lord's vision for obedience. If you have any shortcomings, it is better to see it yourself first so that you can repent and be restored.

In all the times I have visited the Lord in Heaven, I have never experienced Him as the keeper of a long list of "don't." I have experienced Him as the Lord of Grace who is standing with you to help you and guide you. In my experience, He is not really focusing on a list of the things you are not doing. He is not interested in making up and teaching another list of things for people not to do. The Lord is talking about the things He wants you to do for Him and for the kingdom.

The Lord is waiting for people to truly be ready to hear Him and to obey His precepts, guidelines, and commands. I am not judging whether people are ready or not. I do not have a gift to judge others and it would be an act of disobedience for me to do so. It is the Lord who decides. Here is a powerful truth about the love of God! We must have that love to be enabled to be truly obedient to the Lord. Meditate on what Jesus taught about love and obedience!

Jesus answered and said to him, "If anyone loves Me, he will keep My word; and My Father will love him, and We will come to him and make Our home with him. He who does not love Me does not keep My words; and the word which you hear is not Mine but the Father's who sent Me" (John 14:23-24).

Jesus is saying that without obedience you don't really have the fullness of the love of the Father. For many people this comes as shocking news. Some people will outright deny that this is true even though Jesus said it. One woman told me emphatically that God's love is unconditional. I went to the Scriptures to check it out. Nowhere in the Bible does it say that God's love is unconditional. The benefits and blessings of the Lord are conditional on our love and obedience. Remember what John taught in His second letter.

And this is love: that we walk in obedience to his commands. As you have heard from the beginning, his command is that you walk in love (2 John 1:6).

As you reflect on this, remember that obedience is the key to an Open Heaven. According to Jesus, obedience is the key to intimacy with the Father. He also makes it clear that obedience is the key to having The Lord dwell in you. So, I will say it again: "Obedience is the key to the fullness of the Father's love." This is not my idea. I learned it from Jesus.

As you study the teachings of Jesus, you will notice that He clearly states that these teachings are not even His idea. This word is from the Father. Remember what Jesus said in John 12:50, "*And I know that His command is everlasting life. Therefore, whatever I speak, just as the Father has told Me, so I speak.*" It is the same for the Holy Spirit. He does not speak on his own authority. He says only what the Father and the Son tell Him to say. He is our role model for obedience.

However, when He, the Spirit of truth, has come, He will guide you into all truth; for He will not speak on His own authority, but whatever He hears He will speak; and He will tell you things to come (John 16:13).

To me it is clear that we should follow the example of Jesus and the Holy Spirit. I pray for boldness to speak the truth of God in love. Amen? Too many people block their Open Heaven by being disobedient to the Word of God. God will not honor either disobedience or rebellion. He is especially unaccepting of rebellion. He will not violate His own word even to accommodate you. Listen to what He said to the prophet Jeremiah about a man named Hananiah.

Therefore, this is what the Lord says: "I am about to remove you from the face of the earth. This very year you are going to die, because you have preached rebellion against the Lord." In the seventh month of that same year, Hananiah the prophet died (Jeremiah 28:16-17).

Too many people are blocking their own experience of the Open Heaven. I am writing these things to you because I do not want this to happen to you. I want you to live under and receive all the benefits of an Open Heaven. Amen? Those who block their Open Heaven are blocking the flow of blessing and favor in their lives. People wonder why they are not experiencing the things others are testifying to. They need to stop, examine themselves, repent, and get back into obedience if they want to receive the fullness of the blessing and favor of Father God!

I can say confidently that Father God wants to open the heavens for you. I know this because He told me and I believe what He said. So, I appeal to you not to block what He wants to do for you. If you really want to live under an Open Heaven, get into obedience as quickly as possible. Try to always remember what Jesus said in John 10:10 (NIV), *"The thief comes only to steal and kill and destroy; I have come that they may have life, and have it to the full."* The enemy does not plan anything good for you. He only plans to do you great harm. On the other hand, God has a plan to prosper you.

"For I know the plans I have for you," declares the LORD, "plans to prosper you and not to harm you, plans to give you hope and a future" (Jeremiah 29:11).

The Lord has an Open Heaven for you. He wants to open the Floodgates of Heaven and pour out more for you than you can contain. He wants to give you such an abundance that it will spill over into the lives and ministries of others. He even goes beyond these awesome promises and says that He will rebuke the one who devours your resources. It is time to break off the spirit of poverty and release the abundant flow from the Open Heaven. Are we in agreement? Remember the power released by the agreement of the Lord's followers.

Reflect again on what Jesus said in John 10:10b, "*I have come that they may have life, and have it to the full.*" Now look at it as it is written in the Amplified Bible, "*I came that they may have and enjoy life, and have it in abundance (to the full, till it overflows).*" Are you ready for some of the Lord's overflow? Are you ready to receive so much that it will overflow to everyone around you? Then get under the Open Heaven as quickly as you can, and do whatever it takes to stay there.

THE LORD HAS OPENED HEAVEN FOR YOU!

Don't close it back with disobedience. Don't close it by embracing poverty and getting into agreement with the spirit of poverty. Are you ready for an open heaven? Then lift up your hands to the Open Heaven and receive it now! The Lord is not withholding from you. The only one who can block the flow is you. The Lord has decreed a breakthrough for you.

Look at the scriptures below and release these promises over yourself, your family, and your church. Let the words you read aloud release an impartation of the things the Lord has reserved for you. Open you heart to the heavens which have already been opened for you. Allow the Lord to pour out an awesome and abundant impartation to you as your speak it!

IMPARTATION OF A RENEWED MIND

I beseech you therefore, brethren, by the mercies of God, that you present your bodies a living sacrifice, holy, acceptable to God, which is your reasonable service. And do not be conformed to this world, but be transformed by the renewing of your mind, that you may prove what is that good and acceptable and perfect will of God **(Romans 12:1-2).**

But when the kindness and the love of God our Savior toward man appeared, not by works of righteousness which we have done, but according to His mercy He saved us, through the washing of regeneration and renewing of the Holy Spirit, whom He poured out on us abundantly through Jesus Christ our Savior, that having been justified by His grace we should become heirs according to the hope of eternal life (Titus 3:4-7).

PRAYER

Grace, mercy, and peace from God the Father and Christ Jesus our Lord. I thank God, whom I serve with a pure conscience, as my forefathers did, as without ceasing I remember you in my prayers night and day, greatly desiring to see you, being mindful of your tears, that I may be filled with joy, when I call to remembrance the genuine faith that is in you, which dwelt first in your grandmother Lois and your mother Eunice, and I am persuaded is in you also. Therefore I remind you to stir up the gift of God which is in you through the laying on of my hands. For God has not given us a spirit of fear, but of power and of love and of a sound mind. Therefore do not be ashamed of the testimony of our Lord, nor of me His prisoner, but share with me in the sufferings for the gospel according to the power of God, who has saved us and called us with a holy calling, not according to our works, but according to His own purpose and grace which was given to us in Christ Jesus before time began, but has now been revealed by the appearing of our Savior Jesus Christ, who has abolished death and brought life and immortality to light through the gospel, to which I was appointed a preacher, an apostle, and a teacher of the Gentiles. For this reason I also suffer these things; nevertheless I am not ashamed, for I know whom I have believed and am persuaded that He is able to keep what I have committed to Him until that Day. Hold fast the pattern of sound words which you have heard from me, in faith and love which are in Christ Jesus. That good thing which was committed to you, keep by the Holy Spirit who dwells in us (2 Timothy 1:2-14).

PAUSE AND REFLECT

1. In what ways does obedience open heaven for you?

2. What is the Lord telling you to do? Are you ready to obey?

3. What is the Lord's attitude toward rebellion? Give an example!

4. Identify 2-3 things which may be blocking you from the open heaven!

5. List strategies to overcome all things which block you!

CHAPTER 6

GIVING OPENS HEAVEN

KEY 6: GIVING

A few years ago, as I was turning 65, my wife and I decided to retire from fulltime church ministry. The Lord put something new in our hearts. We made a decision to stop working so hard to make a living and to begin to work hard to make a giving. We often say that we retired so that we can work seven days each week for the Lord and to support His kingdom. We didn't know how long the Social Security System could continue. The way the government spends the income from that system for other things makes the future of the program questionable. So, we signed up for Social Security so that we could invest it in the Kingdom. The foundation for our decision was based on what Jesus said in Matthew, Chapter Six:

Do not lay up for yourselves treasures on earth, where moth and rust destroy and where thieves break in and steal; but lay up for yourselves treasures in heaven, where neither moth nor rust destroys and where thieves do not break in and steal. For where your treasure is, there your heart will be also (Matthew 6:19-21).

We quickly learned another powerful truth. You cannot out give the Lord. As it says in John 3:16, "For God so loved the world that He gave...." He has always been a giver and we were created in His image. We are at our best when we do what we see Him doing. As we put this into practice we saw something else. It seemed like the more we gave, the more the Lord released to us. He seems to enjoy watching us give and He blesses us with more seed to sow. Remember: the Lord will do for you what He does for me. He will do for you what He has always done for His faithful followers. He will release this blessing to you the same way He did for Paul. In this venture of giving, we experienced what the Lord taught in Luke, Chapter Six:

Give, and it will be given to you: good measure, pressed down, shaken together, and running over will be put into your bosom. For with the same measure that you use, it will be measured back to you (Luke 6:38).

The Lord began to do some amazing and inspiring things which we received as signs and wonders. We would sow a certain amount into another ministry and within moments that same amount would be given back to us. On one occasion we split the larger gift in two and sowed to two ministries. Someone came to us with two envelopes, each containing the exact amounts we had sown. This person said they had no idea why they split it into two envelops, but the Lord had told them to do this. We immediately understood what the Lord was saying.

The Lord is good all the time and He is faithful to keep all His promises to me and to you.

Sometimes we would sow and the exact amount would suddenly appear back in my wallet. On one occasion, the Lord told me to sow all that I had. I usually keep money in two separate compartments in my wallet. One section I call seed and the other section I call bread. This choice is based on Paul's teaching in 2 Corinthians, Chapter Nine:

Now may He who supplies seed to the sower, and bread for food, supply and multiply the seed you have sown and increase the fruits of your righteousness, while you are enriched in everything for all liberality, which causes thanksgiving through us to God. For the administration of this service not only supplies the needs of the saints, but also is abounding through many thanksgivings to God, while, through the proof of this ministry, they glorify God for the obedience of your confession to the gospel of Christ, and for your liberal sharing with them and all men, and by their prayer for you, who long for you because of the exceeding grace of God in you. Thanks be to God for His indescribable gift (2 Corinthians 9:10-15)!

After I sowed all the seed in my wallet the Lord spoke to me and said, "Now sow the bread!" The Lord had never asked this before. When I heard this, I knew the Lord was going to demonstrate something, but I didn't have any idea what it would be. I obeyed the Lord and sowed the bread. Later, as we were getting ready to drive home from the conference, my wife asked me if I wanted to stop and eat on the way home. I told her that we could do that if she had some money, but I had sown all I had. I opened my wallet to show her. To my surprise, I had five crisp new one hundred dollar bills in the seed compartment and triple what I had previously had in the bread section. I couldn't wait to sow that five hundred dollars again and see what the Lord would do with the seed.

I am not telling you these stories to say that there is anything special about us. We are simply obeying the Lord. We are trusting Him to provide seed for the sower and bread to eat. He has never let us down. I share this to let you know what the Lord can do for you. Remember the teaching in Revelation 19:10b, *"Worship God! For the testimony of Jesus is the spirit of prophecy."* I am releasing this testimony to you as a prophetic word. If you can receive it, meditate again on the promise of the Lord in Malachi, Chapter Three:

> *"Bring the whole tithe into the storehouse, that there may be food in my house. Test me in this," says the Lord Almighty, "and see if I will not throw open the floodgates of heaven and pour out so much blessing that you will not have room enough for it. I will prevent pests from devouring your crops, and the vines in your fields will not cast their fruit," says the Lord Almighty* (Malachi 3:10-11).

The Lord wants to open the "floodgates of heaven" for you and pour out blessings beyond what you have ever asked or thought! The Lord wants to release multiplication to you. However, you need to sow something for Him to multiply. Remember that a thousand times zero is still zero. But, a thousand times 1 is one thousand. A thousand times 500 is 500,000. This is the mystery of multiplication. This is God's plan to bless and multiply those who are made in His image. God is a giver and we are like Him when we are also givers. Remember John 3:16a,

"God so loved the world that He gave..." He gave more than we could ever ask or imagine!

THE SIXTH KEY TO AN OPEN HEAVEN.

Giving is the sixth key to Open Heaven. Giving is the key to getting into the blessing flow of the Lord. Why is this so hard for us? I believe that the enemy wants to send a spirit of poverty to each of us and tempt us to withhold. The Bible is full of stories of those who withheld and paid a big price for that decision. From murderous Cain to lying Ananias and Sapphira, the outcomes have been the same. Givers are blessed and those who withhold come to ruin. Giving more will always increase the blessing flow of the Lord. Withholding will always block the gift of multiplication. Read aloud this powerful teaching from Malachi! Read it over and over until it sinks deeply into your heart and becomes a part of who you are in Christ Jesus.

Will a man rob God? Yet you have robbed Me! But you say, "In what way have we robbed You?" In tithes and offerings. You are cursed with a curse, for you have robbed Me, even this whole nation. Bring all the tithes into the storehouse, that there may be food in My house, and try Me now in this, says the Lord of hosts, if I will not open for you the windows of heaven and pour out for you such blessing that there will not be room enough to receive it. And I will rebuke the devourer for your sakes, so that he will not destroy the fruit of your ground, nor shall the vine fail to bear fruit for you in the field, says the Lord of hosts (Malachi 3:8-11).

Tragically, this is where many people shut down. They don't have eyes to see this spiritual truth. They don't seem to have spiritual ears to hear what the Lord is saying. Some say this is all Old Testament stuff and we are no longer under the Law. This is false teaching. I know because the Lord has proven it to me over and over. The giving of the tithe predates the giving of the law. Abraham gave a tithe to Melchizedek. Now we know that Jesus is the eternal priest in the order of Melchizedek (Hebrews, Chapter 7), and His faithful followers still give the tithe through Him. He still blesses and multiplies for the Spirit filled believers.

The enemy has brought the spirit of poverty to oppress believers and lead them to compromise in the area of giving. People under the influence of this spirit don't like it when money is mentioned. I grew up among people who had this same spirit and I was taught not to respond to those who asked us to give. It took a work of the Holy Spirit to set me free from this awful spirit which is sent by the enemy to block the flow of God in our lives.

When we minister in the USA and mention giving, we often see people literally grab their wallets or purses and hold them tightly so nothing can get out. They act as if someone is about to pick their pockets. What I have seen over and again is that holding the wallet or purse tightly prevents the flow of God's outpouring into these same containers. People who do this block the fulfillment of the Word of God. They block His promises and they bock their own experience of the open Heaven. Don't block the flow of blessing and favor in your life. Trust the Lord! Trust His Word! Trust those who witness to what He can do with the seed you sow! You can trust these words a little more because I am not taking up a collection. I am giving you the truth from the Word of God.

I am convinced that the Lord wants to open the heavens for you. Don't be like those who block what He wants to do for them. Begin to speak the power of God's Word and break off the spirit of poverty! Begin to confess what the Word of God says! Confess it until it becomes a part of who you are and guides what you do for the Kingdom of God. Another kingdom principle which the Lord revealed to me is that He will out give you every time.

I want to add one thing which is somewhat contro-versial. Many have used or more properly misused this idea in the past in order to get things from other people. They often try to get more than people are able to give. This is never from the Lord. However, I have experienced that sowing when the glory manifests opens the door of Heaven for multiplication. This is a work of the Lord and we have no control over it. However, we always try to sow in the glory. When we do this, it isn't because we want to receive something, but because we are so grateful for what the Lord is doing. We just want to give because He has given to us. The scriptural principle for us is in Matthew 10:8, *"Freely you have received, freely give!"* I know that this is specifically stated about giving your gifts of ministry to others. However, I believe it also applies to your financial resources.

I want to remind you again of what the Lord said in John 3:16, *"God so love the world that He gave...."* God is a giver! You were created in His image. One aspect of that image is for you and me to be givers like our Father in Heaven. I believe that we are only fully operating in the Spirit as we give. We need to get involved in our Father's giving business! Amen? Remember how Paul taught that we are moving from glory to glory into this image.

But we all, with unveiled face, beholding as in a mirror the glory of the Lord, are being transformed into the same image from glory to glory, just as by the Spirit of the Lord (2 Corinthians 3:18).

ANOTHER MYSTERY REVEALED

If you really want to open the heavens, give to Israel. Perhaps you have already learned this and have received this awesome revelation for yourself. But if not, I want to unwrap this mystery for you. I believe that this will be a door opener for you and your church if you begin to give to support ministries in Israel. I am fully convinced that this is a door opener for all who participate in it. Remember what the Lord promised to Israel in Genesis 12:3, "*I will bless those who bless you, and I will curse him who curses you; and in you all the families of the earth shall be blessed.*" Therefore, I choose to bless Israel. I do this first and foremost because it is the right thing to do. At the same time, I am aware that God keeps His promises to bless those who bless Israel. I claim this promise for me, for my family and for my ministry! How about you?

People who don't give, open the door for oppression from a spirit of poverty. The Lord has stated clearly that He wants to rebuke the devourer (spirit of poverty) in your life and in your ministry. However, when you refuse to give, you are saying, "No thank you!" to the Lord. You are saying "No thank you Lord, I prefer the devourer. So, I'll just hold on to what I have until he takes it all." I urge you not to make this mistake. Allow the Lord to open the Heavens for you!

Remember what Jesus said in John 10:10, "*The thief comes only to steal and kill and destroy;*" I don't want to have any covenant with the enemy who would do all this to me. I want to have a covenant of giving with the one who wants to open the floodgates of Heaven and pour out more than I can contain. I want to have a covenant with the one who promises to rebuke the devourer! How about you? Many people, who refuse to give, are letting the enemy continue to steal, kill and destroy. It is time for a change.

Giving opens the door for this change. It releases the power of God to rebuke the devourer and restore everything you have lost. In fact, it releases the power of multiplication. When you catch the thief, he must restore seven fold. Could you use a seven fold return on all you have lost? Then listen again to the promise! It is a mystery which has now been revealed to all of Gods people: Giving -- opens the floodgates of Heaven.

For I know the plans I have for you, declares the LORD, plans to prosper you and not to harm you, plans to give you hope and a future. Then you will call upon me and come and pray to me, and I will listen to you. You will seek me and find me when you seek me with all your heart (Jeremiah 29:11-13).

God has a plan for you and it is an awesome plan. He does not want to harm you or take away from what you need. He wants to prosper you. He wants you to be filled with hope for a future of more than adequate provision. He wants you to draw near to Him so that He can draw near to you. He has an open heaven for you. He has promised and He is faithful to keep His promises. He will rebuke the one who devours your resources. Will you trust Him? If your answer is "Yes!" then let's break off the spirit of poverty right now! Remember 1 Corinthians 14:32, *"And the spirits of the prophets are subject to the prophets."* Take authority over your spirit right now and command that the spirit of poverty be cast off and for your spirit to be set free to operate in all the glory the Lord has given to you! Amen?

Are we in agreement about breaking off this spirit of poverty? There is great spiritual power in agreement. We often miss the release of this power, because we do not come into agreement with other believers. I want to come into agreement with you in this area. Remember what Jesus said in John 10:10b, "*I have come that they may have life, and have it to the full.*" This is powerful and I am in agreement with you for you to have the fullness of the blessing of the Lord. Meditate on this verse. Read it aloud over and over. Then do the same with the way it is written in the Amplified Bible: "*I came that they may have and enjoy life, and have it in abundance (to the full, till it overflows).*" I am ready for overflow! How about you?

THE LORD HAS OPENED HEAVEN FOR YOU!

After the Lord has done so much to open Heaven for you, don't make the mistake of closing it up again with your disobedience. Don't close it by embracing poverty or by allowing the spirit of poverty to oppress your spirit. Are you ready to live and minister under an Open Heaven? This is the Lord's plan for you. Remember, His plan is to prosper you! May you line up all your plans with His plan! May you experience all that the Lord wants to pour out for you! May you live in the overflow from Heaven!

Are you ready for an Open Heaven? I believe that this is something the Lord wants us to impart to others. I believe that we can place a claim on the promises in the Word of God and live with expectation that they will manifest. I believe that every promise in the Word of God is for me. I believe that every promise in the Word is for you. If you are a born again believer in Yeshua ha Messiach, this is your inheritance!

Are you ready to receive it? Then open up your spirit to receive it right now! Open up your spirit to receive everything the Lord has for you. Many people need to have their minds renewed and their souls transformed to operate in this level of anointing. Below I share the promise from the Word. Receive it as an impartation for you, your family and your church. Read it aloud over and over until it truly becomes yours! Receive it right now and let it grow stronger and stronger in you and let it release its power for you! Amen and Amen!!!

IMPARTATION OF RENEWED MIND

And do not be conformed to this world, but be transformed by the renewing of your mind, that you may prove what is that good and acceptable and perfect will of God (Romans 12:2).

PRAYER

Now may He who supplies seed to the sower, and bread for food, supply and multiply the seed you have sown and increase the fruits of your righteousness, while you are enriched in everything for all liberality, which causes thanksgiving through us to God. For the administration of this service not only supplies the needs of the saints, but also is abounding through many thanksgivings to God, while, through the proof of this ministry, they glorify God for the obedience of your confession to the gospel of Christ, and for your liberal sharing with them and all men, and by their prayer for you, who long for you because of the exceeding grace of God in you. Thanks be to God for His indescribable gift (2 Corinthians 9:10-14)!

PAUSE AND REFLECT

1. Are you working hard to make a living or working hard to make a giving?

2. How does your attitude influence the flow of God's prosperity?

3. Make a list of the times the Lord has given to you!

4. Do you give with joy or agony?

5. Has the Spirit of poverty been robbing your resources?

6. How do you break free from this oppressive spirit?

7. Have you blessed Israel and received a blessing from the Lord?

8. If your answer is "Yes" how did it manifest for you?

CHAPTER 7

PRAYER OPENS HEAVEN

KEY 7: PRAYER

During His earthly ministry, Jesus said and did some very awesome things. His words often amazed and even confounded the best minds in Israel. He did not teach as others in His day taught. He taught with authority – an authority which caught people off guard. His authoritative teachings often penetrated the barriers which had been placed in their minds by so much false teaching and so many manmade doctrines. The quote from Jesus in John, Chapter Fourteen still amazes and stirs my spirit and soul every time I read it and meditate on it.

> *I tell you the truth, <u>anyone who has faith in me</u> will <u>do what I have been doing</u>. He will do <u>even greater things</u> than these, because I am going to the Father. And I will do <u>whatever</u> you ask in my name, so that the Son may bring glory to the Father. You may ask me for <u>anything</u> in my name, and I will do it (John 14:12-14).*

Jesus is our role model and example for all things spiritual. I have learned to trust everything He says whether

I fully understand it or not. In the passage above Jesus releases one of the most profound truths in the Word of God. He said that those who have faith in Him will do what He did and even greater things. How is that possible? Read the Gospels again and note down all the things our amazing and awesome Lord did during His earthly ministry. How can we do things like that? It is a great mystery and each of us has been called to be on a quest to learn the height, depth, width, and the length of the powerful teachings of our Lord Jesus. Join with me in a journey of discovery into the deep things of the Spirit.

PRAYER: A KEY TO OPEN HEAVEN

While keeping in mind this teaching of Jesus about doing greater things, consider this: While He prayed, Heaven was opened. Think about it! If Jesus did it, then you and I can do it! Do you believe this? We need to build up our faith to the point where we can accept and live by every word of the Lord. If He said it, it is the absolute truth! Now, look at the passage below, read it aloud, and speak this truth into your heart. You may need to read it aloud over and over for it to fully sink into your spirit.

When all the people were baptized, it came to pass that Jesus also was baptized; and while He prayed, the heaven was opened. And the Holy Spirit descended in bodily form like a dove upon Him, and a voice came from heaven which said, "You are My beloved Son; in You I am well pleased (Luke 3:21-22).

Does Heaven open when you pray? I believe that it should happen each time you pray. However, you may need to learn how to use a new type of prayer. You may need to learn to pray like Jesus prayed. The disciples once asked Jesus, *"Lord, teach us to pray, as John also taught his disciples."* (Luke 11:1) As you meditate on this truth, begin to envision the Lord doing even greater things through you and through your ministry for the Kingdom. Take some time to meditate on the powerful promises in the passage below. Again, it is important to read these things aloud so that they can sink deeply into your spirit and your soul.

> *Ask, and it will be given to you; seek, and you will find; knock, and it will be opened to you. For everyone who asks receives, and he who seeks finds, and to him who knocks it will be opened. Or what man is there among you who, if his son asks for bread, will give him a stone? Or if he asks for a fish, will he give him a serpent? If you then, being evil, know how to give good gifts to your children, how much more will your Father who is in heaven give good things to those who ask Him* (Matthew 7:7-11)!

This is a season for the release of supernatural blessing and favor. This is the season of the Open Heaven! By faith begin to build up your expectation that the Lord will release a powerful flow of all the good things your heart desires. Believe that He will open the floodgates of Heaven and pour out more than you can contain. As you lift your faith level higher and higher, you open your spirit to receive more.

Trust the Lord and His promise that you will receive what you ask for. Believe that the good things of the Lord which you are seeking in your spirit are available and will be given to you. Believe that every spiritual door you knock on will open up and release more and more blessing and favor to you, your family, and your church. Believe and receive! Think about what Jesus said to the

Roman Centurion, "*...as you have believed, so let it be done for you.*" (Matthew 8:13) Now that you are ready to believe and receive, meditate on the passage below and take hold of it by faith in your spirit!

> *Every good gift and every perfect gift is from above, and comes down from the Father of lights, with whom there is no variation or shadow of turning. Of His own will He brought us forth by the word of truth, that we might be a kind of firstfruits of His creatures* (James 1:17-18).

Many people we meet as we travel around the world in ministry seem to have missed the message in James 1:17. They keep confessing all the bad things which have come to them. Some even say it is from the Lord. We need to renew our minds and transform our souls so that we can truly receive the fullness of the blessing of the Lord. Father God is the giver of every "good gift" and of every "perfect gift." Too many people are expecting the wrong things from the Lord. Remember what Jesus said to the two blind men in Matthew 9:29, "*According to your faith let it be to you.*" If you receive in accordance with your faith, what will you receive?

The Lord told me to write a book for intercessors (*Restoring Foundations*). As the Lord began to reveal what He wanted me to put into that book, one of the things He revealed to me was: real intercessors must pray in accordance with His Word and His Will. Then I began to notice that there are some very powerful prayers in the Word of God. I understood that if I pray these same prayers, they will always be in accordance with His Word and His Will. This is why I am using so many of them at the end of the chapters in this book.

I began to get really excited about praying the prayers in the Bible. One of the prayers I had used as a discipline several years ago is found in the first chapter of the book of Ephesians. I paraphrased this prayer into the first person and prayed it daily for many months. The Lord was so good to release all these things to me. I recommend this as a prayer discipline for you in this season. We all need supernatural wisdom and revelation to deal with all the deception released in the world today.

I keep asking that the God of our Lord Jesus Christ, the glorious Father, may give you the Spirit of wisdom and revelation, so that you may know him better. I pray that the eyes of your heart may be enlightened in order that you may know the hope to which he has called you, the riches of his glorious inheritance in his holy people, and his incomparably great power for us who believe. That power is the same as the mighty strength he exerted when he raised Christ from the dead and seated him at his right hand in the heavenly realms (Ephesians 1:17-20, NIV).

As I was writing this chapter, I began praying this for you the reader. I prayed over and over for you to receive the Spirit of wisdom and revelation. Think about all the spiritual things this prayer can release for you. Now, you pray it so that you can know Him better! Amen? What can be more important to us in this age than to know the Lord better? Oh! How I desire this for you and for me.

But there is more. You pray this so that your spiritual eyes may be opened. This is so important in this generation. I want to be part of the generation of Jacob (Psalm 24) that seeks His face. I want to be able to see what I am seeking. How about you? Are you seeking His face?

Do you want to see Him for yourself now? Then pray this prayer over and over.

This prayer is so powerful and it opens Heaven so that the Lord can pour out more and more spiritual blessings for you. He wants to pour out so much that it will spill over into the lives of all those around you. So, pray this over yourself daily so that you can *"know the hope to which He has called you."* This is such an amazing concept! The Lord wants you to know something very special. He wants you to know "hope." But, not just any hope. He wants you to know the hope of your calling. Amen? May you pray for it to manifest daily and may the Lord give you the righteous desires of your heart!

The Lord has so much for you and He wants you to understand it better and better. Therefore, I encourage you to pray this prayer continuously so that you can *"know the riches of your inheritance."* As I sought for this, I noticed that there is a great deal of confusion in the Body of Christ about our inheritance. From an early age I was taught that I would receive my inheritance after I died.

One day it dawn on me that this is not how an inheritance works. You don't have to die to get it. You get an inheritance because someone else died. Jesus died on the cross to release your inheritance for you. This inheritance is for both now and later in Heaven. Amen? Think about what Jesus said to the disciples in Luke, Chapter Eighteen. Read aloud the passage below over and over and let it sink into your spirit so that you can know the truth about your inheritance.

So He said to them, "Assuredly, I say to you, there is no one who has left house or parents or brothers or wife or children, for the sake of the kingdom of God, who shall not receive many times more in this

present time, and in the age to come eternal life"
(Luke 18:29-30).

The Lord wants to release more power to us than we can comprehend. Would you like to receive that? Look again at that prayer in Ephesians 1:17-20. Think about the power the Lord has made available to you for your ministry in the Kingdom. It is like the power the Lord released to raise Jesus from the dead. Wow! That is some really amazing power, and it is for you! It is resurrection power!

Yeshua prays this way. You were given this prayer in the Word of God so that you could begin to move in power in the same way he did. Remember, you can do what Jesus did. Let it really sink in what Paul is saying. This great power is for you. Remember what Jesus said in Matthew 10:8, *"Heal the sick, cleanse the lepers, raise the dead, cast out demons. Freely you have received, freely give."* The prayer in Ephesians, Chapter One is designed to release this power into your ministry. What kind of power? Resurrection Power!

First of all recognize that this is about your resurrection to eternal life. You are to freely give what you have already received. You have received the resurrection from the dead before you die. Wow! Isn't that amazing! What do we have to fear? We have died with Christ already. We were buried with Him by Faith and we are raised with Him by the same faith in His promise. Now is a good time to read the passage below and let it sink into your spirit and your soul.

And God raised us up with Christ and seated us with him in the heavenly realms in Christ Jesus, in order that in the coming ages he might show the incomparable riches of his grace, expressed in his kindness to us in Christ Jesus (Ephesians 2:6-7).

Good news! You have already been raised with Christ! You were seated with Him in the heavenly realms! Notice that this is written in past tense which means it has already happened. It isn't merely something to hope for at some point in the future. It is something to receive by faith right now. Amen? During one of my third Heaven visits, I wanted to find my seat. The Word says that I was seated with Him. So, obviously I have a seat in Heaven and I wanted to know where it was located. So I asked and I received an answer from the Lord. Do you believe that you have a seat in Heaven? If you do, then why not go and visit your seat once in a while!

Meditate on this awesome truth: You were raised up with Christ and seated with Him in Heavenly places. Why would The Lord do this? I believe that it is because he wants to show the incomparable riches of His grace! We are actually living in the "coming age" Paul was writing about. This is the time to receive the fullness of all these promises. This is the time to build up your most holy faith so that you can appropriate everything He has promised for you.

All of these things are given so that He can demon-strate the fullness of His grace to you! As I continued to study the book of Ephesians and pray the prayers I found there, I discovered something else. I like the way Paul introduces this to us with the phrase "But now in Christ." Now that you are in Christ Jesus, you are living under an Open Heaven. This is not a passive promise. The Lord just keeps pouring out more and more for you and for me! Amen? With this basic understanding, study the passage below and soak in all that it releases for you. By faith, take hold of the second part which begins with "But now...!"

...remember that at that time you were separate from Christ, excluded from citizenship in Israel and

foreigners to the covenants of the promise, without hope and without God in the world. But now in Christ Jesus you who once were far away have been brought near by the blood of Christ (Ephesians 2:12-13).

All of these teachings are about citizenship in the kingdom of God. This is about a new hope. No matter how far away you may be or how far away you were in the past, you have been brought near by the "blood of Christ." You are no longer a stranger or an alien. You have been drawn into a new and powerful relationship with the Father, the Son, and the Holy Spirit! All I can say is, "Thank you Lord! You are so amazing and wonderful! My heart is filled with gratitude for all you have done and for all you will do in the future!" Do you believe this? Then, begin now to claim the promises for yourself. Fully receive the promise below:

For he himself is our peace, who has made the two groups one and has destroyed the barrier, the dividing wall of hostility, by setting aside in his flesh the law with its commands and regulations. His purpose was to create in himself one new humanity out of the two, thus making peace, and in one body to reconcile both of them to God through the cross, by which he put to death their hostility. He came and preached peace to you who were far away and peace to those who were near (Ephesians 2:14-17, NIV).

As the old preacher used to say, "Think about it!" Jesus is our Shalom! Receive this with the full meaning of the word Shalom. It means that you have received everything you need and as a result you experience His peace. Now the dividing wall of hostility has been set aside. In the New King James Version, it says that this wall has been broken down. It has been destroyed forever. There is no longer any separation for those who are in Christ Jesus! Hallelujah! Thank you Lord!

Think about it! He brought Shalom to both Jewish and Gentile believers. This is so important! In unity, we are a new creation! Some people have erroneously taught that we can have unity apart from others. That is impossible! In the past, others have taught that we can only have unity with people who believe exactly as we believe. This is clearly not what the Word of God is teaching. The Lord is bringing people who are very different in faith, in practice, and in personality together in a new kind of unity in Him.

NOTICE: This unity is the Key to experiencing an Open Heaven! This unity is the key to releasing you for Third Heaven Visitation. *"For through him we both have access to the Father by one Spirit."* (Ephesians 2:18) It is critically important for us to have this unity with Jewish believers. My wife and I have been committed to this for several years. We made it a priority in our lives and ministry to visit Israel every year. We want to pray for them and minister to them. We pray for healing and they get healed. It is not about us! It is about what the Lord wants to do for His Chosen People.

There is a powerful anointing right now for people in Israel to be healed. Remember what the word says: "Jews need a sign." So the Lord is releasing healings, signs and wonders in order to bring them back to Him through Yeshua ha Messiach! This is wonderful, and the Lord allows us to be His instruments for this purpose, and He blesses us for every act of obedience. Therefore, we want to establish relationships with Jewish believers in order to continue to experience the Open Heaven.

When Jewish believers and Gentile believers come together in unity, the Lord opens the heavens. I am not claiming that this is my way! I am declaring that it is the

Lord's way. It is His Word and it is in accordance with His will. When Jewish believers and Gentile believers come together in unity with Jesus something powerful happens. This is one of the main keys to an Open Heaven. I am repeating this so that it will sink in for you as it has for us. It is in this unity, that the Holy Spirit is released to give us access to the Father in Heaven.

However, it doesn't end here. The Lord always has more for us. Catch the full meaning of what Paul wrote in Ephesians 2:19, "*Consequently, you are no longer foreigners and strangers, but fellow citizens with Gods people and also members of his household,*" Did you get it? In this unity, you are a citizen of the Kingdom of God. You are no longer an alien. You are a member of His family. Isn't that an awesome thought? Think about all this unity opens up for you. You now have access to His household in Heaven. Heaven is your new home. If it is your home, you have access to it. If it is your home you have permission to visit. If it is your home, you can abide there forever! Amen?

As if this is not enough, the Lord gives more. You are not only welcome in His home, but He comes to dwell with you. Ephesians 2:22, "*And in him you too are being built together to become a dwelling in which God lives by his Spirit.*" This unity between Jewish and Gentile believers is one of the powerful keys to fully experiencing the promise of the Word that you are the Temple of God. Think about it! He dwells in you! That is an awesome thought. But be aware, along with this awesome promise comes an awesome responsibility.

Do you not know that you are the temple of God and that the Spirit of God dwells in you? If anyone defiles the temple of God, God will destroy him. For the temple of God is holy, which temple you are (1 Corinthians 3:16-17).

This responsibility may be what hinders many people from becoming all that the Lord wants them to be and from experiencing all that the Lord has for them. People have told me that they do not want this level of intimacy with the Lord because they simply do not intend to change their lifestyle. In this age, they value the things of the flesh more than the things of the spirit. Many believe that they can ignore all of this from the Lord and still go to Heaven when they die. I am not so sure. How can you be in Christ and be in disobedience and rebellion. It just doesn't work that way.

Jesus answered and said to him, "If anyone loves Me, he will keep My word; and My Father will love him, and We will come to him and make Our home with him. He who does not love Me does not keep My words; and the word which you hear is not Mine but the Father's who sent Me" (John 14:23-24).

You cannot receive the fullness of the Father's love unless you love Jesus and obey His word. The Father will not bless disobedience. He will not reside in a house of rebellion. The Lord wants so much more for you and He is appealing to you in Christ Jesus to answer His calling on your life. You have been invited to move with Him in the Heavenly places. Don't miss that opportunity!

The Lord commanded me to impart third Heaven visitation to people. Not all of them have experienced it. I once asked the Lord why this is and He answered me, "It is my grace!" I was a little stunned by this remark. So, I asked for wisdom and revelation to understand what He meant. I was told that when we visit in Heaven the Lord will tell us things to do. Many people are not ready and willing to obey the Lord. If they are told to do something in Heaven directly by the Lord and they disobey, judgment will come quickly. The Lord doesn't want to give judgment in this age of grace. So, He is waiting for them to become ready to obey.

Then He told me that there are some things He will not allow in Heaven. If you are holding on to these things it will block your experience of the open Heaven. He said that bitterness, unforgiveness, strife and rebellion will not be allowed in Heaven. Before you seek third Heaven visitation ask yourself if you are ready to obey whatever the Lord tells you to do? If not, then begin to renew your mind and transform your soul until that willingness emerges. If you are ready to obey, then I release this impartation to you. This is also in the book, "*Beyond the Ancient Door*."

IMPARTATION
FOR THIRD HEAVEN VISITATION

I received this impartation and anointing during a visit to the third Heaven. Just before this experience began I had been praying, "Lord, I am available! Use me any way you desire!" I asked for an anointing on my hands for healing and impartation of fire. Then, I felt the fire of God coming on me. It was covering my arms and hands from my elbows down to the tips of my fingers.

I was then taken to a place in heaven which I had not visited before. Jesus was standing in front of me and to my right side. Directly in front of me, I saw a very long line of people which looked like a prayer line. My first thought was, "Why would anyone in heaven want a prayer from me? I am still living on the earth and they have already entered their eternity in heaven." The Lord answered my thoughts and told me this was not a prayer line. I was relieved until the Lord said that it was an impartation line. My first thought was, "Why would anyone in heaven need or even want an impartation from me?" The Lord knew my thoughts and answered, "It's not for them! It's for you! I am going to teach you how to impart a renewed mind!" This was something totally new to me. I had never heard of an impartation for the renewing of the mind, and it seemed like a strange concept to me.

The Lord instructed me to lay hands on people in a way I had never used before (see the graphic image below). The palms of my hands were over their eyes with my fingers around the sides of their heads (over their ears) and both thumbs were touching the center of their foreheads. I didn't get my hands positioned correctly the first couple of times and the Lord took my hands and formed them into the correct posture. When I did this, I felt intense power flowing from Him, through me, and into those receiving the impartation. Each time I did this, I saw the Lord Jesus put His hand on top of their heads. His hand looked like it was on fire and I could feel the heat on my hands while I was still releasing the impartation. I knew that the important part of this was His touch and not mine. I was told to be obedient and He would do the rest.

Then the Lord said, "I am releasing an impartation for the renewal of minds! I am releasing an anointing on you to pass this impartation on to others! I will renew, refine and purify the minds of those who will lift their masks and humble themselves to receive it!" One by one the people in the line walked up in front of me as the Lord instructed me for this anointing. I had to continue to do this for everyone in that very long line.

I wish I could tell you that I immediately responded with willingness to obey. However, that is not what happened. I had to go through a type of renewing of my mind so that I would be able to be obedient to the Lord for this anointing. When I came back from heaven, I shared this with my wife. When I finished telling her what happened, she said, "Well, when you hold your hands like that, it sort of look like a dove." I looked at my hands and agreed that they did have a shape similar to a dove, but I was fairly sure this was not what it meant.

Then, I admitted to her that I was struggling with the idea of offering it to people because this is a very personal way of touching people. I was unsure if anyone would really want to be touched this way. When I do this my hands cover almost their whole face. I was really having difficulty with the idea that people would want me to do that.

The Lord has been very faithful to answer my prayers for discipline and admonishment, and He answered that prayer in a very short period of time. I was lifted back up into heaven. I was standing in the same spot with Jesus in front and on my right side. There was the impartation line again, but it looked longer this time. Being brought back like this on a second visit really startled me. Then the Lord announced firmly, "Re-training!"

I was told to go back through the entire procedure. One by one, people came forward for the impartation. Each time, Jesus' hand was on top of their heads releasing a refining and purifying fire. Each time, the Lord made sure that I was holding my hands correctly. Then, the Lord stepped in front of me and looked directly in my eyes. Then, He gave me a very stern order. He said, "I am telling you to do this! Do you think you can do it now?" Wow! That was a very memorable experience. I knew that there was only one correct answer. I stood at attention and said a firm "Yes Sir! I can do that!"

At this point I took a chance and asked the Lord a question. "If I am anointed to do this for others, who will do it for me?" I really wanted the Lord to impart this to me, but I didn't ask directly. I share this to make a point. If you want something from the Lord, ask directly! Tell Him what you want! The Lord answered my question, but not in the way I expected. He said, "I have uniquely created you to impart this to yourself. If you will hold your hands up with your palms facing you and cross your arms, your hands will form the same pattern as when you impart to others." I did this, and it worked. So, I imparted it to myself. I still longed to receive it directly from the Lord, but had to wait until November to receive it on another visit to heaven. It only came after I had been obedient to this command many times.

Near the end of the first conference in Korea, I shared this experience and command from the Lord. I was still struggling with the issue of the personal nature of this impartation, and told the congregation that I would under-stand if they didn't want to be touched this way. I was also aware that many Korean people do not like for others to touch their heads and you need to have permission before doing this. When I invited those who would like to have the impartation to come forward, I was shocked again. It was like a stampede. Everyone came running forward and I was almost knocked over from the rush. I was the speaker for several conferences back to back for two weeks and had the same response from every dif-ferent congregation.

After giving this impartation at the last church conference, a very good Korean friend of mine who also happens to be a Torah scholar came up and asked, "Do you know what that is?" As he asked this, he had his hands together the way Jesus had taught me. I admitted that I didn't fully understand it, but was being obedient to the Lord. He said, "This is the Aaronic blessing. This is how Aaron held his hands while blessing the people. It forms the Hebrew letter "shin" which looks similar to a letter "w" in English. It has two very powerful meanings. It stands for the name of God and consuming fire." Wow! This really caught my interests and initiated an extensive search for the full meaning of this Hebrew blessing.

As I studied from several Hebrew websites and various scholars, I came to understand that this Hebrew character has five primary meanings all of which directly relate to imparting a renewed mind.

1. It is the primary character in the word "Shaddai" which can be translated as either God Almighty or God of the Mountains (See Genesis 17:1, Psalm 68:14, 91:1). This word derives from the root word "shadad" which means to destroy or completely overpower.

2. It is the primary character in the word "esh" or Fire. The Hebrew character "shin" is often written with flames coming from all three upper points of the letter. Another interesting and powerful idea is that it is always related to the Hebrew word "iysh" meaning man. (See Ezekiel 10:6-7) We were created to carry His fire.

3. It is the primary character in the Hebrew word "shoov" meaning repent in the sense of having a complete change of thinking. In other words, it is pointing to a renewing of the mind.

4. It is the primary character in the Hebrew word "shalom" meaning peace, wholeness and wellness.
5. It is the primary letter in the word "Shekinah." This word means the glory of God as when the cloud appeared to the people in the wilderness, in the tabernacle, in the Temple, and on the mount of transfiguration. It is also speaking about the column of fire by night which led, protected, and resided with the Children of Israel.

This study led me to the Aaronic blessing given in the sixth chapter of the book of Numbers. At first, I was caught up in the words of this profound blessing. I was in awe of the Lord giving a command for this to be done. As I meditated on this, I received another huge revelation. We have the words, but not the pictures which can be found in many Hebrew writings about this blessing. While in Israel, I found some of these books and to my amazement Aaron's hands were positioned exactly as the Lord had taught me. Think about it as you study and appropriate this blessing into your spirit.

"Adonai said to Moshe, 'Speak to Aharon and his sons, and tell them that this how you are to bless the people of Isra'el: you are to say to them,

'Y'varekh'kha Adonai v'yishmerekha,
[May Adonai bless you and keep you.]
Ya'er Adonai panav eleikha vichunekka.
[May Adonai make his face shine on you and show you his favor.]
Yissa Adonai panav eleikha v'yasem l'kha shalom.
[May Adonai lift up his face toward you and give you peace.]'
(Numbers 6:22-26, CJB)

At first, I stopped with verse twenty six. However, the Holy Spirit drew my attention to the next verse in this chapter. I was a little stunned when I considered verse twenty seven in this particular translation. The way it was written opened a whole new line of understanding for me. The Lord said to Moshe, *"In this way they are to put my name on the people of Isra'el, so that I will bless them."* (Numbers 6:27, CJB) The Lord is putting His name on us! He is doing this to bless us! Hallelujah! Thank you Lord! After seeing this clearly for the first time, I went to Ezekiel, Chapter Nine.

> *Now the glory of the God of Israel had gone up from the cherub, where it had been, to the threshold of the temple. And He called to the man clothed with linen, who had the writer's inkhorn at his side; and the Lord said to him, "Go through the midst of the city, through the midst of Jerusalem, and put a mark on the foreheads of the men who sigh and cry over all the abominations that are done within it"* (Ezekiel 9:3-4).

I received by revelation that the man clothed in linen will place the Hebrew character "shin" on the foreheads of all those whose hearts are aligned with Father God's heart. Part of this revelation came during that August trip to Korea. In one location, I had a strange experience at breakfast the morning I planned to release this impartation during the evening service. I began to feel a very strong pulse in my thumbs. This was strange and I couldn't remember ever feeling this before and commented to my wife about it. I said, "I can feel my pulse in my thumbs! I never felt that before!" As quickly as this came out of my mouth, I heard the Lord say, "That's not you pulse! It's mine! When you impart to people, you are putting my heartbeat into them and their hearts will begin to come into synchronization with my heartbeat! They will begin to love what I love and care about the things which I value!" Wow! This was getting deeper and deeper! Then the Lord led me one step further. The Holy Spirit spoke to me about what He had revealed in the book of Revelation, Chapter Seven.

> *Then I saw another angel ascending from the east, having the seal of the living God. And he cried with a loud voice to the four angels to whom it was granted to harm the earth and the sea, saying, "Do not harm the earth, the sea, or the trees till we have sealed the servants of our God on their foreheads." And I heard the number of those who were sealed. One hundred and forty-four thousand of all the tribes of the children of Israel were sealed (Revelation 7:2-4).*

By revelation from the Holy Spirit, I came to understand that the mark on their foreheads will be the same Hebrew character "shin." Now, I understood more fully what Numbers 6:27 was referring to. This impartation was putting the seal of God on people when they truly allowed Jesus to renew their minds with His fiery hand. This was literally putting the name of God, "Shaddai" on the foreheads of His people.

When the Lord first commanded me to release this impartation, I was completely unaware of its meaning. I had never seen or heard of any of this. I had to be obedient first. The Lord used my obedience to open the way for the rest of this revelation. After receiving it, I realized that this gift from the Lord is an extremely precious anointing for me to release these things to others. I have been doing this ever since the Lord's command first came to me. Now, I release it to you.

AN IMPARTATION

To impart this to yourself, simply lift your hands up in front of your face with your palms facing toward you. Cross your hands so that they come together as in the figure above. Place your hands with your palms over your eyes, your fingers toward or over your ears and with your thumbs on your forehead. Remember it is not about what is in your hands. It is about obedience and about the fire in the hand of Jesus.

Now, speak the words of Numbers 6:22-27 over yourself. As you speak, this awesome blessing over yourself, begin to sense the fiery hand of Jesus on your head. You will know the renewing of your mind is working when you can feel the heat from the Lord's hand on your head. Receive it by faith! In addition to the blessing, I always proclaim something like the paragraph below:

Begin to feel the fiery hand of Jesus on your head. I decree that your spiritual eyes are being opened wide so that your seer anointing will increase and you can begin to see into the third Heaven. Your spiritual ears are being opened fully so that you can hear the voice of the Lord speaking to you. Begin to hear Him saying to you, "Come up here!" I impart to you the heartbeat of the Lord so that your heart will come into sync with His, and you will begin to love what He loves and value what He values. Feel the fire as the Lord refines and purifies your mind.

I do this for myself daily because I am convinced that this is a key to being able to visit in the third heaven. We have so many doctrines of man and so much of the spirit of religion in us that doubt will come back over and over. However you can take charge of your spirit. You can take steps every day to stand by faith on the Lord's promises. Remember what Paul said:

I beseech you therefore, brethren, by the mercies of God, that you present your bodies a living sacrifice, holy, acceptable to God, which is your reasonable service. And do not be conformed to this world, but be transformed by the renewing of your mind, that you may prove what is that good and acceptable and perfect will of God (Romans 12:1-2).

Stand in faith that the work which the Lord began in you will be completed. Read again (aloud if possible) Peter's description of what happened on the day of Pentecost and make it yours. Renew your mind over and over until you know with certainty that you have been anointed to see visions, speak prophetic words, and visit the third heaven often. Amen?

But Peter, standing up with the eleven, raised his voice and said to them, "Men of Judea and all who dwell in Jerusalem, let this be known to you, and heed my words. For these are not drunk, as you suppose, since it is only the third hour of the day. But this is what was spoken by the prophet Joel: 'And it shall come to pass in the last days, says God, that I will pour out of My Spirit on all flesh; Your sons and your daughters shall prophesy, Your young men shall see visions, Your old men shall dream dreams. And on My menservants and on My maidservants I will pour out My Spirit in those days; And they shall prophesy. I will show wonders in heaven above and signs in the earth beneath: Blood and fire and vapor of smoke. The sun shall be turned into darkness, and the moon into blood, before the coming of the great and awesome day of the Lord. And it shall come to pass that whoever calls on the name of the Lord shall be saved'" (Acts 2:14-21).

Throughout the scriptures, God has been very clear about His intentions. In the last days, He plans to pour out His Spirit on all flesh. In this outpouring, it should be the norm that His modern-day disciples experience and report visions, dreams, and words of prophecy. The fulfillment of this prophecy is rarely seen in denominational churches today. Those who have visions and give words of prophecy have been at best marginalized and at worst called heretics by the mainstream church. Some teach that the dispensation, prophesied by Joel and explained by Peter, has come and gone.

The absence of visions, dreams, and prophecies in the church is tragic. How will we hear from the Lord except by the methods He has established? Is He known only in the scriptures or do we have a personal God who interacts with His people? Has God left us to our own programs, designs, and visions or is He still in charge; leading His people with a cloud by day and a column of fire at night?

On the other hand, many of those who have developed an intense desire for the fulfillment of this prophesy have found themselves running from prophet to prophet, visionary to visionary, and dreamer to dreamer seeking to hear the Word of God. In each conference or sermon, they hear a Word, pick up some new vocabulary, and become like parrots. They are merely repeating the words given by another. At best they become pale shadows of the latest movement.

I believe that, in these last days, God is calling all believers to come forth and receive the messages of the kingdom directly from him. He wants you to visit in Heaven so that you can hear directly from Him. He wants you to hear what He is saying so that you can say it. He wants you to see what He is doing so that you can do. Meditate on the passage below so that you can receive the fullness of this teaching. Believe it and receive it so that it will manifest for you and your ministry.

> *But the anointing which you have received from Him abides in you, and you do not need that anyone teach you; but as the same anointing teaches you concerning all things, and is true, and is not a lie, and just as it has taught you, you will abide in Him (1 John 2:27).*

PRAYER

> *Now I pray to God that you do no evil, not that we should appear approved, but that you should do what is honorable, though we may seem disqualified. For we can do nothing against the truth, but for the truth. For we are glad when we are weak and you are strong. And this also we pray, that you may be made complete. Therefore I write these things being absent, lest being present I should use sharpness, according to the authority which the Lord has given me for edification and not for destruction (2 Corinthians 13:7-10).*

PAUSE AND REFLECT

1. In what ways have you been doing the things Jesus did?

2. In what ways have you done even greater things?

3. What kind of prayers open heaven?

4. Does Heaven open when you pray? Why or Why not?

5. If you receive in accordance with your faith, what will you receive?

6. What does the Lord promise for those who give to Israel?

7. What can you do to position yourself for visits to Heaven?

CHAPTER 8

SEEKING HIS FACE OPENS HEAVEN

KEY 8: SEEKING HIS FACE

As I make my joyous journey through the Word of God several times each year, I am drawn to one particular person more than anyone except the Lord Jesus. I am drawn to the stories of King David. I love to read them over and over. For a long time I was unaware of why these passages had such a strong pull on my spirit. David was the youngest of eight brothers and no one thought that he would ever amount to much. They kept him out with the sheep when Samuel came seeking the next king. Surely no one would choose a person like David. After all, he was the least among his brothers. He didn't look like kingly material. But, the Lord has a different way of choosing. The Lord looks into the heart.

Samuel had a challenge understanding how the Lord chooses people. He tended to look on the outside appearances. That is why he liked the choice of Saul so much. He was tall, strong, and handsome. He looked like a king, and people were immediately drawn to him. As we all know, that choice didn't work out very well. Saul did not have a heart totally dedicated to the Lord. He was not seeking the Lord with an intense desire to obey and to live in His presence. The word of the Lord came to Samuel and he explained the difference between Saul and David this way:

And Samuel said to Saul, "You have done foolishly. You have not kept the commandment of the Lord your God, which He commanded you. For now the Lord would have established your kingdom over Israel forever. But now your kingdom shall not continue. The Lord has sought for Himself <u>a man after His own heart</u>, and the Lord has commanded him to be commander over His people, because you have not kept what the Lord commanded you" (1 Samuel 13:13-14).

Talking to the king this way was a very risky move on Samuel's part. It was dangerous to speak a message like this to someone who had the power of life and death in His hands. This gives a glimpse of Samuel's heart. He had a heart to obey the Lord even if it meant giving up his life. His heart was totally dedicated to the Lord and he spoke what the Lord instructed him to say. In spite of this, he had not yet come to understand how the Lord chooses by looking at the heart. He was very impressed with David's oldest brother, Eliab. Like Saul before him, Eliab looked like a king, however, the Lord knew his heart. He was not the right man for the job. We get a glimpse of Eliab's heart later in 1 Samuel 17:28 when he rebukes David for asking about the giant from Gath known as Goliath. Eliab had a heart of pride.

David had other brothers who looked almost as impressive as Eliab. But the Lord instructed Samuel, *"Do not look at his appearance or at his physical stature, because I have refused him. For the* LORD *does not see as man sees; for man looks at the outward appearance, but the* LORD *looks at the heart.*" (1 Samuel 16:7) This is still a challenge for us today. We often select leaders because of their appearance and their ability to speak well in public. This hasn't worked out very well for us either. In this season of darkness and deception, we need the spiritual gift of discernment. We need to be gifted to see into the heart of those we select to be our leaders.

The Lord chose the one who had previously been rejected by his own father as well as by his older brothers. They didn't see any real potential in David. Many of us have faced that same situation. People have looked at us and judged us by our outward appearance. If they didn't see something attractive or impressive about us, they discounted us and moved on to someone else. But, this is not how the Lord looks at people. When our reading of the Word of God takes us to the book of Acts, we see what the Lord was seeing in David.

And when He had removed him, He raised up for them David as king, to whom also He gave testimony and said, "I have found David the son of Jesse, a man after My own heart, who will do all My will." From this man's seed, according to the promise, God raised up for Israel a Savior—Jesus— after John had first preached, before His coming, the baptism of repentance to all the people of Israel (Acts 13:22-24).

The Lord was seeking a man who was more like Himself. He was looking for a man who was able to live and serve more like the Lord had created him to be. The Lord was looking for someone who (on the inside) looked more like

His own image. Would you like to have people say this of you? In the end, would you like for the description of your life to be – he/she was a person after God's own heart. I love the way the Lord describes David. The Lord also honored David by mentioning his name more than 1,000 times in the Bible. The number varies depending on which translation you use.

We get another glimpse of what the Lord was seeing when we read about David's desire to have the ark of God moved to Jerusalem. David wanted to have the presence of the Lord close to where he lived. He wanted the presence of the Lord close to where decisions were made and challenges were faced. David want to have the Lord nearby all day every day. How is your heart toward God? Are you seeking His presence where you live, work, and minister? What are you doing to make it happen for you like it happened for David?

So they brought the ark of God, and set it in the midst of the tabernacle that David had erected for it. Then they offered burnt offerings and peace offerings before God. And when David had finished offering the burnt offerings and the peace offerings, he blessed the people in the name of the Lord (1 Chronicles 16:1-2).

David set up a tent and placed the ark of God in the tent. He arranged for worship and praise to be lifted up 24 hours a day, seven days a week. His fervent worship of the Lord caused many problems for him. He was rejected by his own wife who resented his extravagant worship of the Lord. She thought he had made a foul of himself by being totally caught up in praise. There is still a price to be paid for those who give their entire heart and loyalty to the Lord. You may be rejected by those closest to you.

Each person in each generation has to choose whom he/ she will love most.

David rebuked his wife, Michal, for condemning his behavior. Obviously the Lord also rebuked her, because she was not fruitful for the rest of her life. We need to learn a lesson from this Biblical account. It is dangerous to criticize and condemn others who worship and serve the Lord differently than we have chosen to do. We need to be careful about judging people for the intensity of their devotion and the exuberance of their praise. We may bring a curse on ourselves as Michal did and be fruitless for the rest of our lives.

> So *David said to Michal, "It was before the* LORD, *who chose me instead of your father and all his house, to appoint me ruler over the people of the* LORD, *over Israel. Therefore I will play music before the* LORD. *And I will be even more undignified than this, and will be humble in my own sight. But as for the maidservants of whom you have spoken, by them I will be held in honor." Therefore Michal the daughter of Saul had no children to the day of her death* (2 Samuel 6: 21-13).

David was not perfect. Like many of us, he made some really bad choices and did some terrible things. However, these mistakes, failures and sins never broke his relationship with the Lord. He had a heart to seek the Lord even when he had sinned. When he was made aware of his sin, he immediately repented, humbled himself, went into the Lord's presence and sought to restore the relationship. This is what it means to have a heart for the Lord.

Meditate on the psalm of David which first appears in the book of First Chronicles. Begin to worship the Lord like David worshipped Him. David's heart for extravagant and intense worship of the Lord is one of the reasons I love the Psalms which he wrote so much more than the others. More than any of the other writers, his praise is alive with pure awe and admiration for the Lord. Take David's advice and become a person who seeks the Lord with all your strength. Be a person who seeks the Lord's face forever.

> *Glory in His holy name; Let the hearts of those rejoice who seek the Lord! Seek the Lord and His strength; seek His face evermore! Remember His marvelous works which He has done, His wonders, and the judgments of His mouth* (1 Chronicles 16:10-12).

Many of David's Psalms give profound revelation about how we can draw near to the Lord and experience Him drawing near to us. Listen to what David tells you in Psalm 73:28, *"But it is good for me to draw near to God; I have put my trust in the Lord God, that I may declare all Your works."* It is indeed good to drawn near to the Lord. This teaching transcends the gap between the Old Testament times and the New Testament times. Consider David's challenge and the one given by James, the brother of Yeshua ha Messiach:

> *Draw near to God and He will draw near to you. Cleanse your hands, you sinners; and purify your hearts, you double-minded. Lament and mourn and weep! Let your laughter be turned to mourning and your joy to gloom. Humble yourselves in the sight of the Lord, and He will lift you up* (James 4:8-10).

At one point in my pilgrimage with the Lord, I thought that James was giving a rebuke in this passage. However,

I now see that he was restating what had been written by David centuries before. He was telling us again how we can dare to enter into the Lord's presence. We need to have clean hands and a pure heart in order to be close to the Lord. You can wash your hands, but how do you cleanse your heart?

The truth is that you cannot make either your hands or your heart clean on your own. This is a work of the Lord Jesus alone. We are only clean when we are washed in the blood of the Lamb. We are only presentable to the Lord when we wear the garments he has provided for us. Look back at the description of this clothing in Chapter Four. The Lord has provided the garments, but it is our responsibility to put them on. Once we are clothed in the garments provided by Yeshua ha Messiach, we can answer the challenging questions in Psalm 24.

Who may ascend into the hill of the Lord? Or who may stand in His holy place? He who has clean hands and a pure heart, who has not lifted up his soul to an idol, nor sworn deceitfully. He shall receive blessing from the Lord, and righteousness from the God of his salvation. This is Jacob, the generation of those who seek Him, who seek Your face (Psalm 24:3-6).

We are seeing the emergence of this generation in our times. More and more people have experienced a great heart hunger to seek the Lord's face. Are you a part of this generation? Are you sensing an overwhelming hunger for more of Him? I have been growing increasingly hungry and thirsty for more of Him, His presence, and His glory with each passing year. As I receive more, something unexpected happens. I don't become satisfied and content to stay where I am. I begin to feel the emergence of an even greater hunger and I want to press in for more. How about you?

> *Hear my voice when I call, O LORD; be merciful to me and answer me. My heart says of you, "Seek his face!" Your face, LORD, I will seek. Do not hide your face from me, do not turn your servant away in anger; you have been my helper. Do not reject me or forsake me, O God my Savior* (Psalm 27:7-9, NIV).

There are at least two powerful lessons in this passage. First, hear the admonition of David to "Seek his face!" Begin to press in for it. Seek it more intensely each day! You need to stir it up in your spirit. You need to fan it into a flame and let it burn with such intensity that you cannot help but seek Him. Remember Paul's instruction to Timothy in 2 Timothy 1:6 (NIV), "*For this reason I remind you to fan into flame the gift of God, which is in you through the laying on of my hands.*" If you haven't had hands laid on you to give you the fire and hunger for Him, seek someone who can impart this to you. If you can't find anyone, impart it to yourself.

The second teaching David gives in the passage from Psalm 27, is his personal testimony. Whether you choose to do it or not, listen closely to what David says, "*Your face, Lord, I will seek.*" It releases great spiritual power when we strongly affirm our "I will!" to the Lord. Something of the enemy's hold on us is broken when we decree, "I will!" So, speak it aloud! Say with great strength and will, "I will seek His face! I will seek the face of the Lord with all my heart!" After you do this, do it again. Keep doing it until it becomes your nature to do it. Keep doing it until you are a man or woman after God's own heart! Keep doing it until you cannot imagine any other way for your life!

As I write these words for you, I am feeling that hunger welling up inside my own heart. I pray that you are also experiencing an increase in your hunger for him. This hunger and the act of seeking His face with all your heart are powerful keys to experiencing an Open Heaven! The more you draw near to Him the closer He comes to you. I pray that you will accept the challenge of the writer of Hebrews in the passage below. Read it aloud until it becomes yours.

Therefore, brethren, having boldness to enter the Holiest by the blood of Jesus, by a new and living way which He consecrated for us, through the veil, that is, His flesh, and having a High Priest over the house of God, let us draw near with a true heart in full assurance of faith, having our hearts sprinkled from an evil conscience and our bodies washed with pure water (Hebrews 10:19-22).

Remember who the Lord is! He is "Jehovah Shammah" the Lord who is present. He is not far away from anyone who is seeking Him. He is not far from you! The greater your desire for Him the more you will experience Him as the one who is present in your life, your family, and your ministry. Like the prophet Ezekiel, I want to rename my city and my home, "The Lord is there!" (Ezekiel 48:35) He is indeed Jehovah Shammah! Hallelujah! Thank you Lord for opening Heaven and drawing near to us! Thank you for being present in all our times! Thank you for being with us to celebrate during all the good times! Thank you for being with us when life brings a challenge and we seem to be left alone by all the people we love! Thank you for letting us know that we are never alone! You are always with us to love, support and comfort us! Thank you Lord!

You are so awesome and so good all the time! Thank you for being my Jehovah Shammah! Amen and Amen!!!!

PRAYER
(The Temple of God is in your heart)

Yet regard the prayer of Your servant and his supplication, O Lord my God, and listen to the cry and the prayer which Your servant is praying before You: that Your eyes may be open toward this temple day and night, toward the place where You said You would put Your name, that You may hear the prayer which Your servant makes toward this place. And may You hear the supplications of Your servant and of Your people Israel, when they pray toward this place. Hear from heaven Your dwelling place, and when You hear, forgive. If anyone sins against his neighbor, and is forced to take an oath, and comes and takes an oath before Your altar in this temple, then hear from heaven, and act, and judge Your servants, bringing retribution on the wicked by bringing his way on his own head, and justifying the righteous by giving him according to his righteousness. Or if Your people Israel are defeated before an enemy because they have sinned against You, and return and confess Your name, and pray and make supplication before You in this temple, then hear from heaven and forgive the sin of Your people Israel, and bring them back to the land which You gave to them and their fathers. When the heavens are shut up and there is no rain because they have sinned against You, when they pray toward this place and confess Your name, and turn from their sin because You afflict them, then hear in heaven, and forgive the sin of Your servants, Your people

Israel, that You may teach them the good way in which they should walk; and send rain on Your land which You have given to Your people as an inheritance (2 Chronicles 5:19-27).

PAUSE AND REFLECT

1. In what ways are you a man or woman after God's own heart?

2. What are some ways you can seek His face in worship?

3. How do you draw near to Him on a regular basis?

4. What price have you paid for your extravagant worship of the Lord?

5. What price are you willing to pay to draw near to Him?

CHAPTER 9

CHILDLIKE FAITH OPENS HEAVEN

KEY 9: CHILDLIKE FAITH

Several times the Lord has allowed me to watch His interaction with children in Heaven. I am amazed and in awe with each of these lessons from the Lord. The first thing I noticed was His deep love for each child. I can see in their faces and activities that they fully understand this love and feel completely comfortable and safe in His presence. Next I noticed how much He enjoys being with the children. He often plays with them with childlike abandon. He smiles and laughs aloud with everything they do together. This has given me a new perspective on what Jesus said about our need to become more like little children.

Then Jesus called a little child to Him, set him in the midst of them, and said, "Assuredly, I say to you, unless you are converted and become as little children, you will by no means enter the kingdom of heaven. Therefore whoever humbles himself as this little child is the greatest in the kingdom of heaven" (Matthew 18:2-4).

I want to have this kind of faith which is based totally on love and trust for the Lord. How about you? In our development, most of us as children longed to grow up and experience the freedom we thought adults possessed. After we grow up, most of us long for those carefree childhood years of being cared for and nurtured by our parents. We long for the freedom we see in the children. The Lord wants us to understand that this childlike faith is one of the powerful keys which will open Heaven in our lives and in our ministries. Remember, it is all about Him and our relationship with Him. You need to look inside yourself and ask, "Do I have the kind of childlike faith Jesus is talking about?" If not, what are you going to do about it?

I have noticed an amazing thing which most people do. They are always looking for a different time and a different place to find what they need. They seem to believe these things cannot be found where they are right now. They continue to search for another location where they hope to find the freedom and joy they desire? The Lord is telling us to change and experience it now. This is one of the very important keys to an Open Heaven. Don't wait for some time in the future! Don't seek another place! Begin to experience it now! Seek to relate to the Lord more like a little child filled with joy, trust, assurance and love.

When I see the children in Heaven, I feel some of the pain of the parents because they are no longer with them. But, I am assured that the children are happy and safe. They are in the care of one who loves them more than any human being could ever love. He is safeguarding them as they wait to be reunited with righteous parents, brothers, sisters, and friends. This is one of those truths we can handle more effectively when we can see it from the perspective of Heaven. It takes childlike faith to handle the loss of loved ones and to trust them into the care of the Lord.

Human wisdom based on earthly principles can never fully grasp the awesome love and grace of our Lord. He is always ready and willing to lay hands on his children and impart grace, blessing and favor on them. Many adults want to send the children to another room while the grownups meet with the Lord. However, this is not the Lord's desire. One night after I had provided ministry in a meeting, a mother brought her son to share something he had seen in the spirit. He had seen angels and then he saw the Lord. I had also seen these things. So, I asked him to tell me where Jesus was standing and he pointed to the exact spot where I had seen Him. The Lord is manifesting His presence and often it is the children who see it and know it best.

> *Then little children were brought to Him that He might put His hands on them and pray, but the disciples rebuked them. But Jesus said, "Let the little children come to Me, and do not forbid them; for of such is the kingdom of heaven." And He laid His hands on them and departed from there* (Matthew 19:13-15).

May we not be counted among those who would keep the children from the Lord! The Lord is looking for such as these to serve in the Kingdom. He is looking for such as these to reveal the Open Heaven. Wise adults listen to the children and respond spiritually to what they are seeing. Wise adults want to be more like them. They want to be free from the spirit of religion and any other demonic oppression which blocks their ability to see what is happening in the spiritual realm.

167

Keys to Open Heaven

I love to be with children in worship. I am in awe of the love and trust you can clearly see on their faces as they look up in worship to the one who loves them totally. It is always a great joy to hear their testimonies about what they are seeing and the words they hear. They often receive and share powerful words of knowledge and words of wisdom which the Lord is releasing to them. The Lord seems to really enjoy this too, because He so frequently releases some of the most profound revelations through them.

> Then He took a little child and set him in the midst of them. And when He had taken him in His arms, He said to them, "Whoever receives one of these little children in My name receives Me; and whoever receives Me, receives not Me but Him who sent Me" (Mark 9:36-37).

If you want to experience more blessing and favor, take the advice of Jesus. Receive the children in His name. When you receive them, you also receive the Lord Himself. That is wonderful by itself, but the Lord promises even more. When we experience His presence through the children we also receive the Father in our hearts. This is a beautiful description of using this amazing and awesome key to open Heaven.

> So, when he (Judas) had gone out, Jesus said, "Now the Son of Man is glorified, and God is glorified in Him. If God is glorified in Him, God will also glorify Him in Himself, and glorify Him immediately. Little children, I shall be with you a little while longer. You will seek Me; and as I said to the Jews, 'Where I am going, you cannot come,' so now I say to you. A new commandment I give to you, that you love

168

one another; as I have loved you, that you also love one another. By this all will know that you are My disciples, if you have love for one another" (John 13:31-35).

Did you notice that it was when Judas left that Jesus proclaimed, *"Now the Son of Man is glorified, and God is glorified in Him."* Sometimes the unbelieving adults need to leave the room so that the Glory can manifest. When those who doubt and get filled with a rebellious spirit are present, the Holy Spirit doesn't normally manifest. God doesn't like to hang out with the grumblers and the ungrateful people. You may not like to hear this, but it is the truth and you can verify it in the Bible. When disgruntled and rebellious people walk out on the meetings I am leading, I rejoice. I begin to say, "Hallelujah!" I do this because I know that this often precedes a manifestation of the Glory of God.

After proclaiming the glory, Jesus did something very interesting. He began to refer to the adult disciples as "little children." Some might look at that and think He was rebuking them. But, when I read this, I believe that He is giving them a very powerful complement? He had told them previously that they needed to become like "little children" to enter the Kingdom. Now, Jesus seems to be affirming that they have succeeded in being renewed and transformed so that they are now ready to enter the Kingdom of God. I want to say, "Hallelujah!" Jesus speak to us right now! Lord may we hear you referring to us as your "little children!" We are ready to inherit the Kingdom of God and receive it in a way which pleases you. Let our childlike faith bring glory and honor to you and to our awesome Father God! Amen!

My little children, for whom I labor in birth again until Christ is formed in you, I would like to be present with you now and to change my tone; for I have doubts about you (Galatians 4:19-20).

Contrary to this example from Jesus, Paul was not complementing the Galatians by calling them "little children." He was seeing an unhealthy form of immaturity in their beliefs and behaviors. They were being more childish than childlike. He was beginning to doubt their loyalty to the Lord and their ability to maintain sound doctrine. This is made very clear when Paul asks them who had bewitched them. He wondered if they had received the Holy Spirit in vain. This is a powerful rebuke.

O foolish Galatians! Who has bewitched you that you should not obey the truth, before whose eyes Jesus Christ was clearly portrayed among you as crucified? This only I want to learn from you: Did you receive the Spirit by the works of the law, or by the hearing of faith? Are you so foolish? Having begun in the Spirit, are you now being made perfect by the flesh? Have you suffered so many things in vain—if indeed it was in vain (Galatians 3:1-4)?

On the other hand, John (like Jesus) uses the title "little children" as a term of affection. It is as if John thinks of them as his spiritual children. As a spiritual father, John wants to teach them in ways which will help to keep them from sin. He assures them and us that the Holy Spirit is present with the Father and is acting as our advocate. John wants to move them spiritually from focusing on their situation to thinking of the things which are happening in Heaven. Their child like faith was a key to open Heaven and John was seeing it happen. His great desire was for them to see it too. As you study the passage below, let your spirit be lifted up in childlike abandon to see the Holy Spirit interceding for you, your family and your ministry. Wow! What a powerful image! Amen?

My little children, these things I write to you, so that you may not sin. And if anyone sins, we have an Advocate with the Father, Jesus Christ the righteous. And He Himself is the propitiation for our sins, and not for ours only but also for the whole world (1 John 2:1-2).

How many believers today could use a word of encouragement about the situation they are in? How many would like to receive help so that they will not fall back into sin? How many need to hear an encouraging word from time to time? How many would like to hear the Lord providing them with assurance that they have an intercessor and advocate before Father God? Well I want to reassure you that as believers in the Lord Jesus, all of these awesome gifts are available to you. John has a great spiritual gift to be an encourager of the body of Christ. Let him speak into your spirit right now! Let his words, written long ago, release the power of Heaven into your spirit now! I pray that you will let him impart this encouragement to you as you read aloud the passage below and meditate on what it means for you.

I write to you, <u>little children</u>, because your sins are forgiven you for His name's sake. I write to you, fathers, because you have known Him who is from the beginning. I write to you, young men, because you have overcome the wicked one. I write to you, <u>little children</u>, because you have known the Father. I have written to you, fathers, because you have *known Him who is from the beginning. I have written to you, young men, because you are strong, and the word of God abides in you, and you have overcome the wicked one* (1 John 2:12-14).

Here is a powerful truth: Little children are teachable. I believe that this is a powerful revelation about the mystery of little children inheriting the kingdom of God. Are you still teachable? Many adults seem to reject being taught by anyone else. One woman told me that she was too old to be taught anything. She had already learned everything the Lord had to teach her. I thought about what Solomon wrote in Ecclesiastes 4:13 (ONMB), *"Better is a poor and a wise child than an old and foolish king, who will no longer be admonished."* May you always be found to be more like that wise child! Amen!

I do not ever want to get to a place in life where I am no longer teachable. How about you? I want to remain teachable and constantly grow in my knowledge, understanding, and love of the Lord. How about you? I pray and ask the Lord to teach, discipline, admonish and correct me as needed. We need to be as wise as a child who can still receive instruction from the Lord and from others who have more wisdom and experience. We must learn to heed the warning given by Solomon in Proverbs 9:8, *"Do not correct a scoffer, lest he hate you; rebuke a wise man, and he will love you."* Do not become like the scoffer. Search for the word scoffer in Proverbs and learn all these lessons!

It is a spirit of pride which leads us to think we know all we need to know. It is pride which leads us to say we cannot learn from others any longer. Take seriously the teaching in Proverbs 15:32 *"He who disdains instruction despises his own soul, but he who heeds rebuke gets understanding."* We need to be set free from the spirit of pride. We must remain teachable if the Lord is going to bring us higher and higher into the very image of Jesus. John understood this very well when he wrote the following passage.

> *Little children, it is the last hour; and as you have heard that the Antichrist is coming, even now many antichrists have come, by which we know that it is the last hour. They went out from us, but they were not of us; for if they had been of us, they would have continued with us; but they went out that they might be made manifest, that none of them were of us. But you have an anointing from the Holy One, and you know all things. I have not written to you because you do not know the truth, but because you know it, and that no lie is of the truth* (1 John 2:18-21).

John wrote this admonition because they actually knew these things rather than because they didn't know. Sometimes even very wise and well informed people need to hear a teaching again. We need this so that the Word of the Lord will become more solidly implanted into our spirits. Wise people understand the times. We need to stay teachable and alert so that we can be like the sons of Issachar. 1 Chronicles 12:32, "*...the sons of Issachar who had understanding of the times, to know what Israel ought to do...*" Believers today need to understand the times and know what they, their families, their churches and their nations need to do.

Those who are wise know that time is short. John was aware that he was not just living in the last days. According to 1 John 2:18, he tells the "little children" that they are living in the last hour. Understand the times! You are living in the last few moments before the coming of the Day of the Lord. You need to be aware of the time and

173

what the enemy is doing. So that you can also appeal to those who are teachable (little children) and call them into awareness of the times and seasons of the Lord. We are called to waken them to understand what the enemy is trying to do. The enemy is taking people out of our churches and ministries and leading them to teach false things. You must be wise to know the difference between the Spirit of truth and the spirit of falsehood.

We are from God, and whoever knows God listens to us; but whoever is not from God does not listen to us. This is how we recognize the Spirit of truth and the spirit of falsehood (1 John 4:6).

If you are going to live under an open Heaven and experience the good things of the Spirit, you must be wise. You must be firmly rooted in the truth. You must know the source of truth very well and remain teachable at all times. I believe this is what Jesus breathed on the disciples after his resurrection. May the Lord breathe on you right now as He did for them at that moment!

So Jesus said to them again, "Peace to you! As the Father has sent Me, I also send you." And when He had said this, He breathed on them, and said to them, "Receive the Holy Spirit. If you forgive the sins of any, they are forgiven them; if you retain the sins of any, they are retained" (John 20:21-23).

We cannot do the things we are anointed to do unless we have the power and presence of the Holy Spirit with us. We cannot know the truth and see the things which are false unless we have the Spirit of truth as a constant companion. We must get connected with the Lord and stay connected if we are going to accomplish what He has called us to do. We need for Him to be living in the Temple of our hearts. We need to walk and talk with Him every day. We must abide in Him! That is what little children do naturally. They stay close to those they have learned to love and trust.

> *And now, little children, abide in Him, that when He appears, we may have confidence and not be ashamed before Him at His coming. If you know that He is righteous, you know that everyone who practices righteousness is born of Him* (1 John 2:28-29).

We must understand that another aspect of being childlike is that little children can be deceived. We live in a world filled with deception. Most of the sources of teaching today have a world view which does not include God or the Bible. They are working day and night to persuade people to accept their way of seeing things and their methods of working. Although most of these views and methods have been proven wrong or incomplete over and over, they tenaciously hold on and hope to make them work by winning more converts. Sometimes they are more effective missionaries that those in the body of Christ. This should not be!

We must be on guard to prevent this. As little children, we need help to avoid deception and to stay focused on the truth. We need to get a firm grasp on the real truth and stay away from half-truths and lies. All of the forms of deception in the world have the same source at their roots. That ancient enemy is still at work and he is still a liar. In John 8:44, Jesus speaks to those who are teaching things which are false, *"You belong to your father, the devil, and you want to carry out your father's desire. He was a murderer from the beginning, not holding to the truth, for there is no truth in him. When he lies, he speaks his native language, for he is a liar and the father of lies."* Keep this in mind as you study the passage below:

> *Little children, let no one deceive you. He who practices righteousness is righteous, just as He is righteous. He who sins is of the devil, for the devil has sinned from the beginning. For this purpose the Son of God was manifested, that He might destroy the works of the devil. Whoever has been born of God does not sin, for His seed remains in him; and he cannot sin, because he has been born of God* (1 John 3:7-9).

Our task is to teach other "little children" to love and trust The Lord. We are called to teach them to go beyond passively believing the Word of God. They need to put all the commands of Jesus into practice. The main lesson in our walk of faith is love. Remember Paul's first admonition in 1 Corinthians, Chapter Fourteen. He strongly proclaims that the first step is to *"pursue love."* If we have the Love of God the Father and of Jesus Christ in our hearts, we will know the truth and we will do what pleases, honors and glorifies the Lord. Read aloud the passage below and let it sink into your spirit and your soul.

> *My little children, let us not love in word or in tongue, but in deed and in truth. And by this we know that we are of the truth, and shall assure our hearts before Him* (1 John 3:18-19).

The little children we are speaking about here are overcomers. Their love, trust and faith will help them to overcome every obstacle. Little children of faith have the Lord abiding in their hearts. He seems so gentle and kind that they often have to remind themselves that He is also a mighty and powerful warrior king. As little children, we also must always remember that He is a mighty warrior who has already won the greatest battle in human history. Please understand this – "little children" inherit the victory. They share in the spoils of war. They are lifted up and supported to be more than conquerors through Christ Jesus.

You are of God, little children, and have overcome them, because He who is in you is greater than he who is in the world. They are of the world. Therefore they speak as of the world, and the world hears them. We are of God. He who knows God hears us; he who is not of God does not hear us. By this we know the spirit of truth and the spirit of error (1 John 4:4-6).

Little children, understand who the Lord is and what He has done for them! The whole world is under the influence of the "wicked one" right now. You must understand that the only way to stay right with God is to have the wisdom and revelation that the Lord has given to you through the Spirit of Truth. We not only know about Him; we know Him. He calls all the little children to come to Him for blessing, instruction, and favor! Amen?

We know that we are of God, and the whole world lies under the sway of the wicked one. And we know that the Son of God has come and has given us an understanding, that we may know Him who is true; and we are in Him who is true, in His Son Jesus Christ. This is the true God and eternal life. Little children, keep yourselves from idols. Amen (1 John 5:19-21).

Armed with childlike faith, take your stand and embrace the victory which has already been won for you by Yeshua ha Messiach! Believe Him! Trust Him! Seek Him and you will find Him. He will open Heaven for you and call you to be in His presence. He loves to walk and talk with His "little children." I pray that you will also love to spend time with Him every day under the Heaven He has opened for you! Amen!

PRAYER

Grace to you and peace from God our Father and the Lord Jesus Christ. I thank my God upon every remembrance of you, always in every prayer of mine making request for you all with joy, for your fellowship in the gospel from the first day until now, being confident of this very thing, that He who has begun a good work in you will complete it until the day of Jesus Christ; just as it is right for me to think this of you all, because I have you in my heart, inasmuch as both in my chains and in the defense and confirmation of the gospel, you all are partakers with me of grace. For God is my witness, how greatly I long for you all with the affection of Jesus Christ. And this I pray, that your love may abound still more and more in knowledge and all discernment, that you may approve the things that are excellent, that you may be sincere and without offense till the day of Christ, being filled with the fruits of righteousness which are by Jesus Christ, to the glory and praise of God (Philippians 1:2-11).

PAUSE AND REFLECT

1. Do you have the kind of childlike faith Jesus talked about?

2. How does your childlike faith manifest in your life?

3. How can you let your behavior be childlike and open heaven?

4. What can you do to remain teachable?

5. How can you let childlike faith be a source of spiritual strength?

CHAPTER 10

BLESSING OTHERS OPENS HEAVEN

KEY 10: BLESS OTHERS

A s you spend more time with the Lord, you will get to know Him better. In this process you will come to see and appreciate His awesome character. I began to search the Scriptures to learn as much as I could about who He is and what He does. One of the things which impressed me the most in that search was to see more clearly that He is the One who blesses. I like the way He said it to Abraham, *"blessing I will bless you, and multiplying I will multiply you."* Read the passage below aloud over and over until you totally associate blessing with Father God.

> *For when God made a promise to Abraham, because He could swear by no one greater, He swore by Himself, saying, "Surely blessing I will bless you, and multiplying I will multiply you"* (Hebrews 6:13-14).

I really like both blessing and multiplication! How about you? So many people I meet talk on and on about negative things. They often say that the Lord is doing these bad things to them. The only issue many of them have is trying to understand exactly why the Lord is doing these bad things to them. Some people refer to this as "desert theology." Their belief is that the Lord is putting them through all these troubles as tests of their faith or to give them lessons to prepare them for the future.

As I listen to them, I begin to think that they don't know the Lord very well. He is the God who blesses you! He is the God who heals you (Exodus 15:26)! He is the God who provides for you (Malachi 3:10)! He is the God who loves you! The Lord does not do bad things to good people. It is the enemy who desires to steal your blessings, kill you hopes and dreams, and destroy your work for the kingdom of God. John knew the Lord personally during His earthly ministry. Take note of what John says about Him.

And we have known and believed the love that God has for us. God is love, and he who abides in love abides in God, and God in him (1 John 4:16).

This is the God I know and love. He has plans for my life and your life which will bring us hope and a future. He does not plan to harm you or me. If you know the Lord, you will know His love and He will reveal His plans to you. He is the source of good gifts. He is the source of perfect gifts. He is the one who plans to bless you and give you favor all the days of your life. Now, look closely at what Paul says about Him. Read it aloud many times and break off the deception of the enemy about the nature and attributes of God. He is good! He is good all the time! His love and mercy endure forever! Amen?

Blessed be the God and Father of our Lord Jesus Christ, who has blessed us with every spiritual blessing in the heavenly places in Christ, just as He chose us in Him before the foundation of the world, that we should be holy and without blame before Him in love, having predestined us to adoption as sons by Jesus Christ to Himself, according to the good pleasure of His will, to the praise of the glory of His grace, by which He made us accepted in the Beloved (Ephesians 1:3-6).

Now, that is my God! I bless Him for all His goodness and love toward us. We must be careful about what we attribute to Him. Why? Because, according to Genesis 1:27, we were created in God's image ("*So God created man in His own image; in the image of God He created him; male and female He created them.*") Do you believe this? Think about it! If we are created in His image, what kind of people should we be? Are we out to hurt people, test them, and watch them fail? God forbid! We should be people who bless, love, help and provide for others. We should be about our Father's business. He is in the blessing business and so are we when we truly love, obey, and follow Jesus as students and disciples.

Somehow this image of God that we carry got tarnished during the fall in the Garden of Eden. People began to look to themselves and focus on their own needs and desires. They lost their focus on God and on one another. We need to reclaim the part of our image which does the things we see the Father doing. We need to be in the transformation process of becoming more and more like Him. This should be the natural outcome for us as we walk and talk with Him like Adam and Eve did in the Garden. Good news! God is in the restoration business and He wants to help you regain your true identity.

I will make you a great nation; I will bless you and make your name great; and you shall be a blessing. I will bless those who bless you, and I will curse him who curses you; and in you all the families of the earth shall be blessed (Genesis 12:2-3).

Some people read the passage above and think that it is wonderful, but it was only given to Abraham. This false teaching is part of the deception of the world. Tragically it got written into many of the doctrines and teachings of the church. The people who believe the lies of the enemy just don't understand how all the blessings and grace of the Lord could still be available to people today. Since they cannot see it or feel it, they assume no one else experiences it either. Going one step further they begin to teach their false understandings to others and pass them along to another generation.

It is time to break this chain of pain. It is time for people to understand that this is one of the most powerful and destructive works of the spirit of religion. This spirit helps the enemy to accomplish his awful mission. They work together to steal your blessings and rob you of your identity. But, you must look beyond these manmade doctrines and reclaim the true promises in the Word of God. If you have been influenced by the spirit of religion, begin to do that now. Begin by reading the passage below over and over until this promise becomes yours.

Christ has redeemed us from the curse of the law, having become a curse for us (for it is written, "Cursed is everyone who hangs on a tree"), that the blessing of Abraham might come upon the Gentiles in Christ Jesus, that we might receive the promise of the Spirit through faith (Galatians 3:13-14).

183

Our awesome and wonderful Lord Jesus won back for us everything lost in the fall of man. He took the curse upon Himself so that it could be lifted off of you and me! He took the punishment so that we could be free from judgment and condemnation! He did all of this so that you could receive the promise. He did it so that you could inherit the "blessing of Abraham." He did it so that it would be available to both Jews and Gentiles. Let the blessing overtake you and come upon you (Deuteronomy 28:2). Once you fully come under the sevenfold blessing of Abraham, get back into your Father's business – the blessing business! Amen?

Bless those who persecute you; bless and do not curse. Rejoice with those who rejoice, and weep with those who weep. Be of the same mind toward one another. Do not set your mind on high things, but associate with the humble. Do not be wise in your own opinion (Romans 12:14-16).

When we are traveling in Israel, we see many Jewish families who move into the hotels for Shabbat so they can honor the commandment to do no work on the day of rest. I love to watch the young families in the hotels on the evening of Shabbat. During the meal the Father will stand up and go from the oldest to the youngest child laying hands on them and speaking blessing over them. The mother will follow behind the Father doing the same thing.

When I see this I have a desire to see this happening in all the families on Earth. Think about the impact this would have on the world if every child grew up in the blessing of their parents which comes from the blessing of Father God. What if every child grew up knowing that they had the blessing and favor of God on their lives? What if they grew up knowing that everything they put their hand to would succeed? Imagine a world where the blessing and favor of God rested on every single person! This is God's plan, and to me it is awesome!

We were ministering in a church a few years ago where the men were in training to be spiritual leaders in their families. There seemed to be some very big struggles in the families as they adopted this concept from the Word of God. One passage seemed to be at the heart of their struggle. They were looking closely at Ephesians 5:22-24 *"Wives, submit to your own husbands, as to the Lord. For the husband is head of the wife, as also Christ is head of the church; and He is the Savior of the body. Therefore, just as the church is subject to Christ, so let the wives be to their own husbands in everything."* It would have been much better if they had focused more on the passage just after this:

> *Husbands, love your wives, just as Christ also loved the church and gave Himself for her, that He might sanctify and cleanse her with the washing of water by the word, that He might present her to Himself a glorious church, not having spot or wrinkle or any such thing, but that she should be holy and without blemish. So husbands ought to love their own wives as their own bodies; he who loves his wife loves himself* (Ephesians 5:25-28).

As I was preaching on a completely different message, the Lord gave me a revelation about the primary role of men who would be spiritual leaders in their families. When I received this, I immediately thought about those young Jewish families I had seen in Israel. The Lord said that the primary role of the spiritual leader is to bless his wife and children daily. If men would do this with all sincerity and love, most of the problems in marriages and families would go away. The second thing a spiritual leader does is to provide for his family. This goes beyond merely working and bringing home a paycheck. This means that spiritual leaders should be feeding their families in spirit, soul, and body. They should provide for the spiritual, emotional and physical needs of every member of the family. The third role of a spiritual leaders is to protect their loved ones from all danger in both the physical and spiritual realm.

The Lord told me that those who would do these three things would not have any trouble with the other parts of their leadership. I began to teach this during many other meetings. I sought to draw the attention of people to a very powerful part of the Word of God which deals with blessing others. This is Father God's way of blessing. This is how I want to bless others. Study it and make it yours. Practice it in your family. You will be amazed at what this will do for your relationships.

> *And the Lord spoke to Moses, saying: "Speak to Aaron and his sons, saying, 'This is the way you shall bless the children of Israel.' Say to them: 'The Lord bless you and keep you; The Lord make His face shine upon you, and be gracious to you; The Lord lift up His countenance upon you, and give you peace.' So they shall put My name on the children of Israel, and I will bless them"* (Numbers 6:22-27).

I love to speak this blessing over others. It is so powerful. It is the most important part of imparting a renewed mind. The blessing of the Lord does so much for people and they need to receive it. It works best when you do it God's way. Think about it! The Lord said, "*This is the way you shall bless!*" The Lord specifically wanted this blessing to be spoken over His children – the children of Israel. Now that Christ has brought Jew and Gentile together into one new creation, this blessing is for all of us. The Lord wants you to speak it over every member of your family every day!

Have you ever noticed how children want to limit the amount of work it takes to obey their parents? Many adults are still doing this with the Lord. Remember what Peter asked Jesus in Matthew 18:21, "*Then Peter came to Him and said, 'Lord, how often shall my brother sin against me, and I forgive him? Up to seven times?'*" Like most people, Peter was looking for a shortcut to obedience. Be honest, you have wondered the same thing haven't you? I know I have.

But how did Jesus answer Peter (Matthew 18:22)? "*Jesus said to him, "I do not say to you, up to seven times, but up to seventy times seven.* To get a really good understanding of what the Lord meant, study the parable which immediately follows this comment from Jesus. In Hebrew, the number seven is often used like the infinity character in English. Jesus was basically saying you must forgive infinity times infinity times ten. We are called to do a lot of forgiving. Likewise, we are called to do a lot of blessing. The command for blessing goes far beyond family and friends.

> *But I say to you, love your enemies, bless those who curse you, do good to those who hate you, and pray for those who spitefully use you and persecute you, that you may be sons of your Father in heaven; for He makes His sun rise on the evil and on the good, and sends rain on the just and on the unjust* (Matthew 5:44-45).

This is the acid test for our spiritual character. Are we really committed to the Father's blessing business or are we just somewhat willing to bless those we like and love?

Loving your enemies is a huge challenge. Being able to bless those who curse you is a true sign of spiritual maturity. Praying for those who persecute you and spitefully use you is truly Christ-like. But this is one of the powerful keys to open Heaven. When you can actually grow up into this image, you are truly "*sons (and daughters) of your Father in heaven.*" Notice that the Lord sends the blessings of sunshine and rain on all people: the righteous and the unrighteous. This is what it means to be in the Father's blessing business.

> *Finally, all of you be of one mind, having compassion for one another; love as brothers, be tenderhearted, be courteous; not returning evil for evil or reviling for reviling, but on the contrary blessing, knowing that you were called to this, that you may inherit a blessing* (1 Peter 3:8-9).

After the resurrection of Jesus, Peter was restored. His restoration didn't merely make him like he was before. He was better, wiser, and more compassionate than he had ever been in the past. Having gone through the process of falling and being restored he was given a new heart. He was empowered to forgive and bless those who meant him harm, and he called all the believers to move up to a higher level of glory. He challenged people to live in accordance with their calling. Think about it! By blessing others, you are positioning yourself to "*inherit a blessing.*"

I want to inherit the blessing! How about you? I like to get a word from the Lord for someone which releases the seven-fold blessing of Abraham. In other words, the Lord chooses to give them blessing and favor in every area of their lives and ministries. I want to release that to you right now. Are you ready to receive it? Then just reach out and take this powerful blessing from the Lord.

But remember this will bring you into the Father's blessing business. You must be ready, willing and able to take on this challenge. Don't be like the people James describes in the passage below.

> *Out of the same mouth proceed blessing and cursing. My brethren, these things ought not to be so. Does a spring send forth fresh water and bitter from the same opening? Can a fig tree, my brethren, bear olives, or a grapevine bear figs? Thus no spring yields both salt water and fresh* (James 3:10-12).

We cannot truly say that we love the Father unless we are loving and blessing His children. In 1 John 4:20-21 we read: *"If someone says, "I love God," and hates his brother, he is a liar; for he who does not love his brother whom he has seen, how can he love God whom he has not seen? And this commandment we have from Him: that he who loves God must love his brother also."* Did you notice that this is not a suggestion? It is a command from the Lord. Remember who you are and whose you are! How can we have communion with the Lord if we do not bless others?

> *Therefore, my beloved, flee from idolatry. I speak as to wise men; judge for yourselves what I say. The cup of blessing which we bless, is it not the communion of the blood of Christ? The bread which we break, is it not the communion of the body of Christ? For we, though many, are one bread and one body; for we all partake of that one bread* (1 Corinthians 10:14-17).

I want the fullness of the blessing of God. I like the way Paul has assurance of this in Romans 15:29, *"But I know that when I come to you, I shall come in the fullness of the blessing of the gospel of Christ."* When I come to you, I want to come in the fullness of the blessing. So how do we do this? How do we get the fullness of the blessing? Study the passage from Ezekiel and meditate on it to answer these questions!

> *The best of all firstfruits of any kind, and every sacrifice of any kind from all your sacrifices, shall be the priest's; also you shall give to the priest the first of your ground meal, to cause a blessing to rest on your house* (Ezekiel 44:30).

Ezekiel speaks of the *"firstfruits of any kind."* A few years ago, I made a covenant with the Lord to give Him the *"firstfruits"* of every day. I made a firm commitment to begin each day by giving the first part of my time to the Lord. I spend time each morning studying the Word, giving Him praise and glory for all He has done, all He is doing now, and all He will do in the future. I spend time in prayer and meditation. I get face down on the floor and give him my life by praying a variation on James 4:7. I say, "Father God, I submit to you spirit soul and body! All that I am and all that I will ever be, I submit to you! All that I have and all that I ever will have I submit to you! In accordance with your Word and in the Name of Yeshua ha Messiach, I resist the devil and He has no choice but to flee and take all of his works with him! I pray this in the mighty name of Yeshua ha Messiach! Amen and Amen!" Who gets the *"firstfruits"* in your life?

Always remember that we are members of His kingdom of priests. As His priests, we have an important role. We are to bless the Lord. This was the command of the Lord from the beginning. The priests were to minister to and bless the Lord. Then they went out from the Holy of Holies to bless the people. The Lord is calling us back to His ways. I hear him over and over calling us back to the old paths which are the ones He laid out for us from the beginning.

> *The sons of Amram: Aaron and Moses; and Aaron was set apart, he and his sons forever, that he should sanctify the most holy things, to burn incense before the LORD, to minister to Him, and to give the blessing in His name forever* (1 Chronicles 23:13).

Most churches today minister to the people rather than to the Lord. However, our ability to bless others is measured by our ability and willingness to bless the Lord by ministering to Him. After the resurrection of Jesus Christ, the disciples finally got it. Their new behavior is noted in Luke 24:52-53, *"And they worshiped Him, and returned to Jerusalem with great joy, and were continually in the temple praising and blessing God. Amen."*

One of the ways I like to fulfill this role is to speak the words of Psalm 103 to the Lord. I want to give Him glory, honor, majesty and praise every day. Try it! It will do wonders for you relationship with Him. You can begin right now by speaking this blessing aloud. Say it to Him!

> *Bless the Lord, O my soul; and all that is within me, bless His holy name! Bless the Lord, O my soul, and forget not all His benefits: Who forgives all your iniquities, Who heals all your diseases, Who redeems your life from destruction, Who crowns you with loving-kindness and tender mercies, Who satisfies your mouth with good things, so that your youth is renewed like the eagle's* (Psalm 103:1-5).

Our praise and worship are a blessing to God. I ask every morning to hear what heaven is saying today so that I will know what I can do to bless the Father, the Son and the Holy Spirit. This is a powerful key for opening Heaven and having access to the Father. He is inviting us into the "Secret Place of the most high". He is giving us access to the heavens when we love and obey Him. Then He pours out blessings beyond our ability to contain them. I want you to fully receive what the Lord promised in Ezekiel 34:26, "*I will make them and the places all around My hill a blessing; and I will cause showers to come down in their season; there shall be showers of blessing.*" I am ready for a blessing shower! How about you?

Great power is released through the act of blessing. This process of releasing the Lord's blessing over and over can change nations as well as individuals. Proverbs 11:11, "*By the blessing of the upright the city is exalted, but it is overthrown by the mouth of the wicked.*" The Lord is inviting you to take authority over your region by releasing the fullness of His blessing and favor. It is time to get back into the family business. It is time to fully accept our place in the Father's blessing business. Are you ready for it?

Unfortunately, many people are not ready to bless others or to bless the Lord. Some people are filled with bitterness, resentment, pride, strife, and unforgiveness. How can they bless if this is what they have in their heart? They need to purge these things from their hearts before they can release blessing through their mouths. Study the passage below from Mark, Chapter Seven and consider the real meaning of this teaching from Jesus:

He went on: "What comes out of a man is what makes him 'unclean.' For from within, out of men's hearts, come evil thoughts, sexual immorality, theft, murder, adultery, greed, malice, deceit, lewdness, envy, slander, arrogance and folly. All these evils come from inside and make a man 'unclean'" (Mark 7:20-23, NIV).

You can know what is in your heart by listening to the words coming from your mouth. You cannot fake this for very long. You can try as much as you want to control what you mouth speaks, but eventually the things of the heart will come forth. If you have love and blessing in your heart, that is what will come forth. But, if you have evil, cursing, strife, and hatred in your heart, it will eventually come out. You will become known by the things in your heart. Here is the real catch. The evil things you release will come back on you. The curses you try to speak on others will eventually come back on you! Be very careful with what you say!

As he loved cursing, so let it come to him; as he did not delight in blessing, so let it be far from him. As he clothed himself with cursing as with his garment, so let it enter his body like water, and like oil into his bones (Psalm 109:17-18).

Wow! How many people want this outcome? How many people want their word curses to come back upon themselves? Do they want the Lord to withhold blessing and favor the way they withhold them? You probably know someone who has "*clothed himself with cursing as with his garment.*" It isn't pretty when you see it in others. Now you need to examine yourself. If you are in the cursing business, you are doomed to fail. You cannot curse what God has blessed. Learn the lesson of Balaam before it is too late.

On that day they read from the Book of Moses in the hearing of the people, and in it was found written that no Ammonite or Moabite should ever come into the assembly of God, because they had not met the children of Israel with bread and water, but hired Balaam against them to curse them. However, our God turned the curse into a blessing. So it was, when they had heard the Law, that they separated all the mixed multitude from Israel (Nehemiah 13:1-3).

We can avoid this outcome. If we love the Lord, we will obey Him and then the Father will dwell with us and release the fullness of the blessing to us, our families and our churches (John 14:23). I read something in the book of Deuteronomy the other day which really got my attention. I want this outcome for me. I want the Lord to "*command the blessing*" on me! How about you. If you love Him and obey Him this is His promise!

The LORD will command the blessing on you in your storehouses and in all to which you set your hand, and He will bless you in the land which the LORD your God is giving you (Deuteronomy 28:8).

As the Apostle Paul looked back on his years of ministry, he reflected on what he and his ministry team had been enabled to do. You can read this in 1 Corinthians 4:12 (NIV) "*We work hard with our own hands. When we are cursed, we bless; when we are persecuted, we endure it; when we are slandered, we answer kindly. Up to this moment we have become the scum of the earth, the refuse of the world.*" No matter what people threw at them, they gave back blessing. They had taken on the very character and nature of God the Father. Would you like for this to be said about you after your life of service to the Lord comes to a close? It can be. Begin now to follow

Paul's advice found in Romans 12:14, *"Bless those who persecute you; bless and do not curse."*

ONE FINAL ADMONITION

But I say to you who hear: Love your enemies, do good to those who hate you, bless those who curse you, and pray for those who spitefully use you. To him who strikes you on the one cheek, offer the other also. And from him who takes away your cloak, do not withhold your tunic either. Give to everyone who asks of you. And from him who takes away your goods do not ask them back. And just as you want men to do to you, you also do to them likewise (Luke 6:27-31).

PRAYER

May the Lord bless you and keep you,
May the Lord make His face to shine upon you
And be gracious unto you,
May the Lord lift up His countenance upon you
And establish for you Shalom, Shalom, Shalom!
(Numbers 6:24-26)

"So they shall put My name on the children of Israel, and I will bless them." (Numbers 6:27)

PAUSE AND REFLECT

1. Name three ways the Lord has blessed you!

2. How are you participating in the Father's blessing business?

3. What are some of the ways you can bless those around you daily?

4. What are you doing to bless the Father?

5. How can you position yourself to receive the fullness of the blessing?

CHAPTER 11

KEYS WHICH SHUT THE HEAVENS

The main part of the message in this chapter came to me during my meditation time. It was presented to me by the Holy Spirit as a way of looking at things in reverse. Instead of seeing the keys which open Heaven. I saw the keys which tend to close heaven. As I shared this with others, it seemed like an odd way to teach something. Then I remembered that the Lord had led Paul to teach this way in some of his letters. This is not a list of suggestions for thing you should attempt to do. These are things to avoid if you want to live, work and minister under an Open Heaven.

When He had been baptized, Jesus came up immediately from the water; and behold, the heavens were opened to Him, and He saw the Spirit of God descending like a dove and alighting upon Him. And suddenly a voice came from heaven, saying, "This is My beloved Son, in whom I am well pleased" (Matthew 3:16-17).

The Lord reopened what had been closed by the sin and rebellion which had occurred in the Garden of Eden. What an awesome and wonderful Father God who sent His Son to restore us to the Open Heaven. Amen? The Father was "*well pleased*" with Him and the work He was going to do. Remember what Jesus said in Luke 12:32, "*Do not fear, little flock, for it is your <u>Father's good pleasure</u> to give you the kingdom.*" I really like this way of seeing the Father. He has good pleasure when He gives you the Kingdom.

I thought about how the Lord had gone to a lot of trouble and Jesus paid a huge price to open heaven for us. In spite of the pain and suffering, it gave them "*good pleasure.*" How is this possible? It is possible because they love us so much they want to bless us abundantly by giving us the Kingdom. That is true love! What Jesus did is amazing and wonderful. May we be diligent to obey Him so that His awesome work would not be in vain in our lives and ministry!

It will not go well for those who work to close the heavens which the Lord opened at such great cost. Jesus' strongest words of criticism were spoken over those who not only missed the open heaven for themselves but closed it for others. This is how He viewed the outcome of the work of some of the scribes and Pharisees. They were striving so hard to please God, but in all the wrong ways. They were not in the Father's blessing business, and they did not want the "common people" to be blessed. Listen carefully to what Jesus said to them. Do not make their mistake in your own walk with the Lord!

But woe to you, scribes and Pharisees, hypocrites! For you shut up the kingdom of heaven against men; for you neither go in yourselves, nor do you allow those who are entering to go in (Matthew 23:13).

Perhaps you are wondering what you could possibly do to close the door which the Lord has opened. You must remember that you have been given tremendous spiritual authority. *"Behold, I give you the authority to trample on serpents and scorpions, and over all the power of the enemy, and nothing shall by any means hurt you."* (Luke 10:19) Your words and your prayers carry the weight of this authority. You can use it for good or you can use it to do harm. Spend some time meditating on what James said about you and your ability to close the open heaven.

Elijah was a man with a nature like ours, and he prayed earnestly that it would not rain; and it did not rain on the land for three years and six months. And he prayed again, and the heaven gave rain, and the earth produced its fruit (James 5:17-18).

This is such an amazing thought. You have a nature just like Elijah the powerful man of God. God listens to the prayers of His anointed servants. We are no longer to think in accordance with manmade doctrines which would limit our authority in the Kingdom. Be careful what you say and what you pray. You may speak words which close the heavens over you and those to whom you are speaking.

Remember what Jesus says about people who close the heavens! Perhaps you need to examine yourself right now and repent for words you have spoken and prayed which worked to close Heaven. Perhaps you need to ask the Lord to cancel the power released by your words so that the heavens can be opened again. Elijah did both. He prayed and the heavens were closed. Then he prayed and the heavens were opened again. Remember, you have a nature like his and you can do the same things.

I pray that the Lord will keep the heavens open over you and over me. I pray that He will send the Spirit of truth to reveal to us what we need to see in ourselves. I pray that the Holy Spirit will show us what is necessary and then teach us how we should pray. I ask Him to lead us to repentance when that is needed. I pray that He will guide us through the process of restoration so that we can experience the fullness of the blessing and live and minister under the open Heaven! I suggest that you spend some time right now while it is fresh on your mind to do the same thing.

What can we do without the blessing and favor of the Lord? Jesus knew this full well and He understood that while He was in the body He had to deal with certain limitations. In John 5:19, Jesus said, "*Most assuredly, I say to you, the Son can do nothing of Himself, but what He sees the Father do; for whatever He does, the Son also does in like manner.*" Like Jesus, we can do nothing of ourselves. The power and authority in our lives is from Him and it will not work without Him.

We can only do what the Father shows us and anoints us to do for the Kingdom. I want you to fully grasp what the Lord was saying about your ability to do His work. Read the words of Jesus in John, Chapter Fourteen. Read them aloud many times until they become your own. Think about what you can do as a believer. Do the good works of the Lord and avoid the bad.

> *Most assuredly, I say to you, he who believes in Me, the works that I do he will do also; and greater works than these he will do, because I go to My Father. And whatever you ask in My name, that I will do, that the Father may be glorified in the Son. If you ask anything in My name, I will do it* (John 14:12).

Are your words, your actions and your prayers opening the heavens or closing them? Consider carefully what Jesus taught in Luke 12:47, *"And that servant who knew his master's will, and did not prepare himself or do according to his will, shall be beaten with many stripes."* Some people believe that once they say "the sinner's prayer" they are covered and have no further obligation. Remember that Jesus always made the promises of the Kingdom conditional on our love and obedience. We must obey Him in order to open the heavens over us and to keep them open over us and others.

The Lord made this clear from the beginning. One false doctrine that is circulating around the church is that we can ignore the Old Testament because it has been superseded by the New Testament. This is a false teaching. The sacrificial law has been fulfilled, but the Lord is still the same. He has not changed. He is the same yesterday, today and forever. Paul was not talking about the New Testament when he wrote, *"All Scripture is given by inspiration of God, and is profitable for doctrine, for reproof, for correction, for instruction in righteousness, that the man of God may be complete, thoroughly equipped for every good work."* (2 Timothy 3:16-17) What we have as the New Testament had not been recognized as scripture when these words were written.

Then as now, disobedience tends to close the heavens. Outright rebellion will certainly close the heavens over you. We need to take seriously what the Lord has taught about these two character flaws. He will not tolerate disobedience and rebellion in the Kingdom. His words never come back void. So the things He has spoken in the past have not been made void by any new words. I want to serve Him as He wants to be served! I want to worship Him as He wants to be worshipped! I want to be obedient so that the heavens can remain open over me, my family, my church and my ministry! How about you? Looking back at what the Lord has said about obedience is a good thing! Consider what the Lord said in the passage below.

> *And after all this, if you do not obey Me, then I will punish you seven times more for your sins. I will break the pride of your power; I will make your heavens like iron and your earth like bronze. And your strength shall be spent in vain; for your land shall not yield its produce, nor shall the trees of the land yield their fruit* (Leviticus 26:18-20).

I constantly state that I want to have and live under the sevenfold blessing of the Lord. He promised it to Abraham and He passed it on to us through the finished work of Jesus Christ. Refer back to the study on being in the blessing business of the Father. Look again at Galatians 3:13-14 and place a claim on this promise once more. Then make a covenant with the Lord to work and serve in a way which will keep the heavens open.

Have you ever done a study of the things the Lord doesn't like? It is important for us to know what He dislikes and to be keenly aware of what He hates. We need to know the kinds of things which are an abomination to Him. Doing these things will most certainly close the heavens over us. As I searched to understand these things, I found some powerful teachings in the Book of Proverbs. One of the passage I have considered many times is found in Chapter Six:

> *These six things the Lord hates, yes, seven are an abomination to Him: A proud look, a lying tongue, hands that shed innocent blood, a heart that devises wicked plans, feet that are swift in running to evil, a false witness who speaks lies, and one who sows discord among brethren* (Proverbs 6:16-19).

If we do the things the Lord hates, we cannot expect Him to bless it. These are the same things the Lord told me would keep us from visiting in the Third Heaven. Have you longed to visit in the Third Heaven? If so, there may be some things you need to consider. The Lord told me that He does not allow bitterness, unforgiveness, and strife in Heaven. If you have these in your heart you need to take care of this business before you seek a visit with Him. He also told me that the main reason people are unable to visit the Third Heaven is that they are not willing to obey what He commands them to do. Consider the price for falling short of the grace of God.

Pursue peace with all people, and holiness, without which no one will see the Lord: looking carefully lest anyone fall short of the grace of God; lest any root of bitterness springing up cause trouble, and by this many become defiled; lest there be any fornicator or profane person like Esau, who for one morsel of food sold his birthright (Hebrews 12:14-16).

I ask daily for the Lord to send fire to burn out any root of bitterness which may have arisen in my spirit. I ask Him to burn out and remove all unforgiveness and strife so that I can enter into His presence. I want to be with Him now and forever. How about you? Then consider examining yourself to see if any of these things have taken root in you. You need to be set free if you want to live under the Open Heaven. I take very seriously what the Lord teaches us in this twelfth chapter of Hebrews. Consider the following:

But you have come to Mount Zion and to the city of the living God, the heavenly Jerusalem, to an innumerable company of angels, to the general assembly and church of the firstborn who are registered in heaven, to God the Judge of all, to the spirits of just men made perfect, to Jesus the Mediator of the new covenant, and to the blood of sprinkling that speaks better things than that of Abel. See that you do not refuse Him who speaks. For if they did not escape who refused Him who spoke on earth, much more shall we not escape if we turn away from Him who speaks from heaven, whose voice then shook the earth; but now He has promised, saying, "Yet once more I shake not only the earth, but also heaven." Now this, "Yet once more," indicates the removal of those things that are being shaken, as of things that are made, that the things which cannot be shaken may remain. Therefore, since we are receiving a kingdom which cannot be shaken, let us have grace, by which we may serve God acceptably with reverence and godly fear. For our God is a consuming fire (Hebrews 12:22-29).

How will we escape judgment if we disobey? No one has been able to trick or fool the Lord. He knows what is in your heart. When you stand before the judgment seat of Christ, you will not be able to lie or deny what has been in your heart or what you have done to block the open heaven over others. You need to remain ready to meet Him at all times. We have no idea when we will pass from this world into eternity. So, we need to stay prepared for that transition at all times. Remember the promise of the Lord in Luke, Chapter Twelve.

Blessed are those servants whom the master, when he comes, will find watching. Assuredly, I say to you that he will gird himself and have them sit down to eat, and will come and serve them. And if he should come in the second watch, or come in the third watch, and find them so, blessed are those servants (Luke 12:37-38).

After reflecting on these scriptures, I did a study of the things which are an abomination to God. I did this because I took this teaching to heart. I hope you will also take it to heart. I want to know and understand these things which are an abomination to the Lord so that I can avoid them and keep the heavens open.

As I searched, I found another powerful passage in Proverbs 28:9 (ONMB), "*He who turns away his ear from hearing the Torah (Teachings), even his prayer will be an abomination.*" Wow! I don't want my prayers to be an abomination to the Lord. I made a covenant with the Lord a long time ago to stay in His teachings by reading the Word of God every day. I want to know and obey so that I can bring Him the good pleasure of giving me the Kingdom. How about you? To better understand the choices before you, study Deuteronomy, Chapter Eleven.

Behold, I set before you today a blessing and a curse: the blessing, if you obey the commandments of the LORD *your God which I command you today; and the curse, if you do not obey the commandments of the* LORD *your God, but turn aside from the way which I command you today, to go after other gods which you have not known* (Deuteronomy 11:26-28).

Obedience brings the blessings and favor of the Lord. On the other hand, disobedience brings a curse. We have a choice. We can choose to be in the Father's blessing business which will open the heaven over us. On the other hand we can choose to release word curses over others who belong to the Lord. Doing these things will close the heavens over your own life and work. This didn't work out well for Balaam or the Ammonites and Moabites who hired him to curse Israel. We are told in Joshua 13:22, "*The children of Israel also killed with the sword Balaam the son of Beor, the soothsayer, among those who were killed by them.*" Both Peter (2 Peter 2:15) and Jude (Jude 1:11) warn that speaking curses over those blessed by the Lord will not work out well for you.

> *Nevertheless the LORD your God would not listen to Balaam, but the LORD your God turned the curse into a blessing for you, because the LORD your God loves you. You shall not seek their peace nor their prosperity all your days forever* (Deuteronomy 23:5-6).

The same choices have been handed down to us. We must choose whom we will serve and how we will act. If we want to live under an open heaven, we must choose to serve the Lord. The Lord has warned us many times about what will happen if we disobey. He does not want to bring judgment on us during this season of grace. He wants to bless us and shower us with His favor. The only thing which will hold Him back is disobedience and rebellion. He says that He will not only close heaven over us, but He will turn it into bronze. When this happens, the floodgates are closed and everything dries up spiritually.

> *And your heavens which are over your head shall be bronze, and the earth which is under you shall be iron. The Lord will change the rain of your land to powder and dust; from the heaven it shall come down on you until you are destroyed* (Deuteronomy 28:23-24).

I want the open heaven rather than the bronze heaven. How about you? I want the Lord to open the floodgates of heaven and rain down His blessings on you and on me. I want the former and later rains which bring prosperity, long life, health, and favor! I want these things for you also. Trust the Word of God. He will keep the heavens open over all those who will listen and obey. Hallelujah! Thank you Jesus! Amen and Amen!!!

PRAYER

Therefore we also pray always for you that our God would count you worthy of this calling, and fulfill all the good pleasure of His goodness and the work of faith with power, that the name of our Lord Jesus Christ may be glorified in you, and you in Him, according to the grace of our God and the Lord Jesus Christ (2 Thessalonians 1:11-12).

PAUSE AND REFLECT

1. What are some of the things you can change which are closing heaven over you now?

2. What are some of the ways people close heaven over others?

3. Examine yourself to see if there is any disobedience, pride or rebellion in you!

4. Name three things which are an abomination to the Lord!

5. What are some of the ways rebellion can impact the open heaven?

CHAPTER 12

BENEFITS OF AN OPEN HEAVEN

The promises of the Lord are always fascinating to me. I love to read the Word of God and search out all His promises and then claim them for myself. How about you? Are you seeking and standing on the promises of the Lord? When you claim the promises, be sure to include the sevenfold blessing of Abraham! Remember that you have inherited all these blessings and promises if you are in Christ Jesus! For me, it is like a great quest to find hidden treasure. I know that these spiritual things have been hidden from the natural mind but revealed by the Holy Spirit. Look closely at the message below from 1 Corinthians, Chapter Two.

> But the natural man does not receive the things of the Spirit of God, for they are foolishness to him; nor can he know them, because they are spiritually discerned (1 Corinthians 2:14).

As the Holy Spirit gives you access to the Father with the Son (Ephesians 2:18), He also gives you greater understanding of the hidden things of God. There are so many things which you cannot understand in the Word of God unless the Holy Spirit gives you discernment. There are many more things in the spiritual realm which you will never understand unless the Spirit of God reveals them to you. But, there is good news! The Lord has provided a solution for you. Remember Jesus' promise in John, Chapter Sixteen.

> *However, when He, the Spirit of truth, has come, <u>He will guide you into all truth</u>; for He will not speak on His own authority, but whatever He hears He will speak; and <u>He will tell you things to come</u>. He will glorify Me, for He will take of what is Mine and declare it to you* (John 16:13-14).

Some of these things revealed by the Holy Spirit are the benefits of an Open Heaven. I claim the promise in Malachi 3:10, "'... *And try Me now in this,' says the Lord of hosts, 'If I will not open for you the windows of heaven and pour out for you such blessing that there will not be room enough to receive it.'*" He wants to give you more than you can contain! Why? So that it will spill over and flow through you to bless others. Remember the promise in 2 Corinthians 9:8, "*And God is able to make all grace abound toward you, that you, always having all sufficiency in all things, may have an abundance for every good work.*" The Lord loves to supply and multiply! He does it over and over so that out of the abundance there will be all that is needed to carry the gospel to the world.

The blessings of the Lord are much more than just material things. He blesses us in spirit, soul, and body. When the Open Heaven manifests, we experience multitudes of healings of all kinds. When people experience the Open Heaven their souls are transformed and their minds are renewed. In our ministry, we often see people supernaturally receive financial breakthrough. Many times we have seen this manifest purely because it is the Lords good pleasure to give. Bank accounts multiply! Money appears in purses and wallets. These are amazing signs which confirm the truth of the gospel of the kingdom.

At other times, multiplication comes through a gift of wisdom to take the actions which will bring wealth. People love to see and receive these signs and wonders, but there is a higher order of flow from the Open Heaven. I am talking about spiritual things. I am talking about increased intimacy with the Lord. I am talking about wisdom, revelation and understanding flowing into the spirits of people. Lives are changed forever as believers are built up, encouraged and comforted by the presence and power of the Holy Spirit. If you need some of these things, speak in faith and receive them now!

The Open Heaven often begins with it the appearance of angels. Of course this means that in order for you to see it, your seer anointing needs to be activated. Continue to speak to your spirit and activate this anointing so that you can discern these awesome things of the Spirit. Remember the Lord's promise: "Ask and you will receive! Seek and you will find!" Knock and the door of Heaven will be opened for you!

ANGELS SPEAK FROM HEAVEN:

As I went on the adventure of searching the Word of God for revelation, the first account I found of an Open Heaven was experienced by Hagar, Ismael's mother. Heaven was opened for an auditory revelation to her. In her hour of desperation she experienced an Open Heaven and heard the voice of a powerful angel. Angels still come to us in our hours of desperation and they can release powerful and life changing words from the Lord.

In Hagar's case, the angel of God spoke from Heaven to release provision, protection, and destiny.

> *And God heard the voice of the lad. Then the angel of God called to Hagar out of heaven, and said to her, 'What ails you, Hagar? Fear not, for God has heard the voice of the lad where he is. Arise, lift up the lad and hold him with your hand, for I will make him a great nation.' Then God opened her eyes, and she saw a well of water. And she went and filled the skin with water, and gave the lad a drink* (Genesis 21:17-19).

In this initial manifestation, the heavens are opened for the voice of an angel to provide assistance for a boy through a strong revelation to his mother. Mothers hear this clearly! The Lord loves and cares for your children. As he provided for Hagar's son, He will provide for your children! As the Lord opened Hagar's eyes to see His provision, He will open your eyes as well. The Lord has provided living water to nourish and sustain the lives of your children. May the heavens open over you and your children so that you can receive all the Lord has for you! It is in His Word and it is in His will.

> *He will bless those who fear the Lord, both small and great. May the Lord give you increase more and more, you and your children. May you be blessed by the Lord, Who made heaven and earth* (Psalm 115:13-15).

In the Scriptures, I noticed that a short time later heaven opened again for the voice of an angel to be heard by a parent in great distress. This time it came to Abraham. He had been obedient and dramatically demonstrated that he loved the Lord more than the child of destiny who had been given to him supernaturally by the Lord. It is very difficult to fully understand the meaning of this entire account, but we know that it was a foreshadowing of what the Lord would give for us through His Son, Yeshua ha Messiach.

When Abraham reached the end of his spiritual rope and it seemed that all hope was lost, heaven opened. At the last moment, he heard the voice of the Angel of the Lord speaking from heaven. It is important for you to understand that what the Lord did for Abraham He will also do for you. In your darkest hour and at the moment of your greatest need have faith that the heavens will be opened and the Angel of the Lord will speak a word to you! Listen for His voice speaking a blessing from the Lord which will change your destiny, provide exactly what you need, and redeem the time so that you can reach the fullness of your God-given destiny. Think on these things as you read the account of Abraham's Open Heaven experience! Then receive it by faith for yourself, your family, and your church.

And Abraham stretched out his hand and took the knife to slay his son. But the Angel of the LORD called to him from heaven and said, "Abraham, Abraham!" So he said, "Here I am." And He said, "Do not lay your hand on the lad, or do anything to him; for now I know that you fear God, since you have not withheld your son, your only son, from Me." Then Abraham lifted his eyes and looked, and there behind him was a ram caught in a thicket by its horns. So Abraham went and took the ram, and offered it up for a burnt offering instead of his son. And Abraham called the name of the place, The-LORD-Will-Provide; as it is said to this day, "In the

Mount of The LORD it shall be provided." Then the Angel of the LORD called to Abraham a second time out of heaven, and said: "By Myself I have sworn,"' says the LORD, "because you have done this thing, and have not withheld your son, your only son--blessing I will bless you, and multiplying I will multiply your descendants as the stars of the heaven and as the sand which is on the seashore; and your descendants shall possess the gate of their enemies. In your seed all the nations of the earth shall be blessed, because you have obeyed My voice" (Genesis 22:10-18).

At the moment when Abraham needed the Lord the most, heaven was opened and the answer was given. The Lord went far beyond merely providing what Abraham needed at that moment. He restated his destiny! He confirmed His promises given years ago. He released a renewed promise that Abraham would be blessed beyond measure, multiplied beyond human reasoning, protected from enemies, and released in a destiny which would bring blessing to the entire world. Wow! That is a God kind of supernatural moment. Do you need a moment like that in your spiritual walk? Then believe that it is for you and receive it by faith! Amen?

Perhaps you need a supernatural moment with the Lord today. Now is a good time to expect the Lord to break through the darkness and release the light of His Word and the fullness of His blessing on your life. Remember what Jesus said to the Centurion in Matthew 8:13, *"...Go your way; and as you have believed, so let it be done for you."* This promise is also for you! As you have believed, let it be done for you! This promise of Jesus leads me to expect more and to believe for a greater outpouring from the Open Heaven. How about you?

What are you believing that you will receive from the Lord today? Build it up! Build up your most holy faith, and expect the heavens to open for you! Believe that the Lord loves you and is ready to release all you need and more! I want to release an impartation to you right now to receive the things reported in the two verses below. Read them aloud. Believe they are for you and then receive the promise by faith! What they saw and heard, you can see and hear also!

I saw still another mighty angel coming down from heaven, clothed with a cloud. And a rainbow was on his head, his face was like the sun, and his feet like pillars of fire (Revelation 10:1).

And they heard a loud voice from heaven saying to them, "Come up here." And they ascended to heaven in a cloud, and their enemies saw them. **(***Revelation 11:12)*

RESOURCES BECOME VISIBLE

We walk by faith and not by sight! Amen? However, it is a wonderful thing when the things we hope for manifest in the natural. The key to making this happen is to release your faith into your situation so that the Lord may open the heavens for you. Remember the teaching in Hebrews 11:1-2, "*Now faith is the substance of things hoped for, the evidence of things not seen. For by it the elders obtained a good testimony.*" Faith is not a phantom. Faith is substance! It is spiritual substance. So, you need to get your spiritual eyes opened wide to see it. If you are still having trouble seeing in the Spirit, go back to Chapter three and work on releasing it again. Then return to your study of the eleventh chapter of the book of Hebrews and appropriate every promise in this powerful revelation from the Lord!

Faith is truly the evidence of the things we are praying and hoping for. Hope is not enough. It has no substance. You have to add your faith to it for the heavens to open and for the Lord to move into your situation with His redeeming power. We do not walk by sight or by feelings. We walk in faith with an absolute belief that the Lord will do what He says He will do. It is not enough to believe He can. The devil knows that He can. We must rise up to the level of faith which declares that "HE WILL!" Now, take that faith and apply it to the promise below!

Bring the whole tithe into the storehouse, that there may be food in my house. Test me in this, says the LORD Almighty, and see if I will not throw open the floodgates of heaven and pour out so much blessing that you will not have room enough for it. I will pre-vent pests from devouring your crops, and the vines in your fields will not cast their fruit, says the LORD Almighty. Then all the nations will call you blessed, for yours will be a delightful land, says the LORD Almighty (Malachi 3:10-12, NIV).

The Lord encourages you to take this test and see if He will keep His promises. This is an amazing offer from the Lord. His promise is that if you will obey Him, He will open the Floodgates of Heaven for you. He will also pour out more blessings than you can contain. However, the promise doesn't end here. The Lord also promises to rebuke whatever has been stealing your provisions. He will rebuke the enemy who is trying to hinder or reduce the level of your financial blessings. Another promise is that the spiritual fruit of your service in the Kingdom will not fall to the ground and rot. The Lord will prevent all these things from happening to you at the same time that He is flooding you with more!

Could you use this help from the Lord? Would you like for Him to rebuke the one who has been devouring your substance? The Lord decrees, "Trust me in this!" You can trust the Lord. He keeps His word and His word never comes back void. Begin your great adventure of finding all the promises of the Lord for your life, your family, and you ministry and release them by faith. When the Lord is for you, who can be against you! The enemy cannot curse those blessed by the Lord. The enemy cannot steal what the Lord has given to you. Let the Lord rebuke the devourer in your storehouse! Expect by faith that the Lord is about to open the heavens and pour all this out for you. But remember, the key to receiving it is obedience! Amen?

BLESSING AND HEAVEN

When He had been baptized, Jesus came up imme-diately from the water; and behold, the heavens were opened to Him, and He saw the Spirit of God descending like a dove and alighting upon Him. And suddenly a voice came from heaven, saying, "This is My beloved Son, in whom I am well pleased" **(Matthew 3:16-17).**

By now, you have surely noticed that Jesus was an "Open Heaven Carrier." Wherever He went and whatever He did, it was accompanied by the Open Heaven. He heard what the Father was saying and He saw what the Father was doing. Angels ascend from Him while others descended upon Him with more gifts and revelation from the Father. Under the Open Heaven He was transfigured in the presence of three disciples. Moses and Elijah came down through the Open Heaven to chat with Him. Begin your search of the Word of God and find more of these reports.

As you consider this remember what He said in John 14:12, "*Most assuredly, I say to you, he who believes in Me, the works that I do he will do also; and greater works than these he will do, because I go to My Father.*" But, do you truly believe this? Most people believe Jesus said it, but they do not believe it will happen for them. This is not a time for unbelief to steal your promises from the Lord. This is not a time to let the enemy convince you that this was promised to someone else and not to you. This is the time to believe it and receive it so that you can accomplish your mission for the Kingdom of God!

Now is the time to clearly hear what the Lord is saying! I recommend that you study chapters 14-17 of the Gospel of John. I suggest that you do this over and over until you understand fully what the Lord is promising to you. Many people have told me that we cannot receive these things. They say that they were only released to the original apostles. I do not believe this. This is a manmade doctrine which is clearly contrary to the written Word of God. Study the passage below and speak it aloud over and over until it becomes yours!

I do not pray for these alone, but also for those who will believe in Me through their word; that they all may be one, as You, Father, are in Me, and I in You; that they also may be one in Us, that the world may believe that You sent Me. And the glory which You gave Me I have given them, that they may be one just as We are one: I in them, and You in Me; that they may be made perfect in one, and that the world may know that You have sent Me, and have loved them as You have loved Me (John 17:20-23).

Jesus released these promises for all believers in every age. Do you believe that? Then begin to live out that faith! Receive what He promised! Begin to do what He did and expect the season of "greater things" to manifest soon in your life and service for the kingdom of God. Jesus promises that we have access to the heavens. In Matthew 5:3, He said, *"Blessed are the poor in spirit, for theirs is the kingdom of heaven."* In Matthew 5:10, He expanded this to include those who are righteous, *"Blessed are those who are persecuted for righteousness' sake, for theirs is the kingdom of heaven."*

According to Jesus, the kingdom of heaven belongs to us if we are obedient to Him. If it belongs to us, we should be expecting to see it, feel it, and receive it as promised. Amen? Increase your faith so that when you get what you have believed it will be much more than you asked or imagined. Take hold of what Paul was releasing in Ephesians 3:20-21, *"Now to Him who is able to do exceedingly abundantly above all that we ask or think, according to the power that works in us, to Him be glory in the church by Christ Jesus to all generations, forever and ever. Amen."* I want to live at this level – "above and beyond all I have asked or thought." How about you? Then, now is the time to release your faith so that you can receive it.

HEAVEN AS A REWARD

Not everyone who says to Me, "Lord, Lord" shall enter the kingdom of heaven, but he who does the will of My Father in heaven (Matthew 7:21).

If you think through the passage above from the perspective of those who are in disobedience and rebellion, it may seem negative. Instead, begin to think about it from the perspective of those who love and obey the Lord. These are the ones who will inherit the kingdom. This is a promise for you and for me if we will believe it and receive it. Get your spiritual eyes to focus on all the things Jesus taught and see them from the perspective of Heaven.

Now, do the same thing with 1 Corinthians 6:9, "*Do you not know that the wicked will not inherit the kingdom of God?*" Turn this into a positive and you will see that the righteous will inherit the kingdom of God. Now focus on getting into a right relationship with the Lord. Once you have it, you can receive the positive things in the promise. You can receive your inheritance. Changing your perspective to see the positive in all the promises is the way to receive them and experience the Open Heaven. Now look at these things from James' perspective.

> *Listen, my dear brothers: Has not God chosen those who are poor in the eyes of the world to be rich in faith and to inherit the kingdom he promised those who love him* (James 2:5)?

James is teaching this same idea but from a positive perspective. Would you like to receive your inheritance? Years ago I had a friend who was always talking about what he would do when his "ship came in." This was hope without substance. To my knowledge that ship never arrived for him. However, we don't look at things that way. We look through the eyes of faith and see the Open Heaven. Then we can see the truth and the truth will set us free! Get this! Those who live by faith can receive their inheritance now and keep it for all eternity. Hallelujah! Thank you Lord!

At this point I want to repeat something I shared earlier as a way of confirming this promise. As I was growing up in the church, I heard many people teach incorrectly about our inheritance. They taught that it was something we would receive after we died and went to heaven. This didn't make sense to me. You don't get an inheritance when you die. You get an inheritance when someone else dies. Think about it! Jesus died so that you could have your inheritance now and for eternity in Heaven. Receive it by faith now and begin to live under an open heaven so that the Lord can pour out His overflow to you and through you into the body of Christ.

OPEN HEAVEN RELEASES MULTIPLICATION

We serve the God of multiplication. As soon as the Lord created men and women He blessed them with multiplication. Genesis 1:22, *"And God blessed them, saying, "Be fruitful and multiply, and fill the waters in the seas, and let birds multiply on the earth."* He created us in His image and He is a multiplier. Like our Father in Heaven, we should be speaking multiplication into being in our lives and service. If you can receive this teaching, begin now to put it into practice. Release it to yourself and to others. Remember you will be blessed more and more as you bless others.

The Lord released this same command for multiplication to Noah and his sons after the flood: Genesis 9:1, *"So God blessed Noah and his sons, and said to them: "Be fruitful and multiply, and fill the earth."* The blessings and promises given to Adam and his descendants didn't stop with the flood. As you continue your study of the book of Genesis, you will see the Lord releasing the command for multiplication over and over. He gave it to Abraham, Sarah, Isaac and Jacob. He even promised to multiply Ishmael.

Multiplication is released from the heart of God to all his children. The Lord continues to promise this gift to

His people all through the Old and New Testaments. The enemy wants to steal this blessing from you, but it is time for you to take back all the things which have been stolen from you. When you get them back, you need to begin to expect the Lord to multiply them as He has always done in the past. Have you noticed that Jesus was also into multiplication? Study the passage below and begin to accept it by faith!

> *Then He took the five loaves and the two fish, and looking up to heaven, He blessed and broke them, and gave them to the disciples to set before the multitude. So they all ate and were filled, and twelve baskets of the leftover fragments were taken up by them* (Luke 9:16-17).

Did you receive it? Did you move into your anointing of multiplication? Some have asked why they don't see this more often. The answer is usually very simple. They don't really believe it. They may ask for it, but if they don't believe it nothing will happen. Unbelief will block the flow of multiplication in your life. You must get rid of the heart of disbelief or it will continue to rob you of your inheritance. Remember what James taught in the first part of his letter.

> *But let him ask in faith, with no doubting, for he who doubts is like a wave of the sea driven and tossed by the wind. For let not that man suppose that he will receive anything from the Lord; he is a double-minded man, unstable in all his ways* (James 1:6-8).

As you study these promises from God in His Word, is your faith being increased? Begin to ask the Lord for an increase in your faith for these things to manifest for you, your family, and your church. It is your inheritance and the enemy must no longer be allowed to steal these promises from you. As you process these things in your mind and your spirit, look again at what Paul taught about the heart of God and His desire to multiply these things for you. Make this your prayer and speak it aloud over and over. Then watch what the Lord can and will do for you!

Now may He who supplies seed to the sower, and bread for food, <u>supply and multiply</u> the seed you have sown and <u>increase</u> the fruits of your righteousness, while you are enriched in everything for all liberality, which causes thanksgiving through us to God. For the administration of this service not only <u>supplies</u> the needs of the saints, but also is abounding through many thanksgivings to God, while, through the proof of this ministry, they glorify God for the obedience of your confession to the gospel of Christ, and for your liberal sharing with them and all men, and by their prayer for you, who long for you because of the exceeding grace of God in you. Thanks be to God for His indescribable gift (2 Corinthians 9:10-15)!

JUDGMENT FROM HEAVEN

Do not be deceived, my beloved brethren. Every good gift and every perfect gift is from above, and comes down from the Father of lights, with whom there is no variation or shadow of turning (James 1:16-17).

Good things flow from the Open Heaven for those who love and obey the Lord. Good things flow from the open Heaven for those who are not deceived into disobedience and rebellion by the enemy. Perfect gifts are released to those who trust in Him. As you walk with the Lord, you will

223

notice that He does not even make a shadow of turning from you. He is always faithful and true.

However if you choose to live in disobedience and rebellion, something else is promised for you. If you have a rebellious spirit, it will block the flow of the good and perfect gifts which the Lord wants to provide for you. God simply cannot break His Word. He will not do things contrary to what He has said in the past. We need to be delivered from every root of a rebellious spirit. We need to repent of all disobedience and come into a new covenant with the Lord. Otherwise we can expect what Jesus promised in the seventeenth chapter of Luke.

Likewise as it was also in the days of Lot: They ate, they drank, they bought, they sold, they planted, they built; but on the day that Lot went out of Sodom it rained fire and brimstone from heaven and destroyed them all (Luke 17:28-29).

I don't want to see heaven open and pour out the judgment of God on me or any of my family or friends. I don't want fire and brimstone to fall from the open heaven. How about you? This is a teaching and promise from Jesus. It isn't something from the Old Testament which some people have foolishly rejected. It is from the mouth of Yeshua ha Messiach! Read the Gospels again and notice the things the Lord promises will come in the future to those who are disobedient.

And there will be great earthquakes in various places, and famines and pestilences; and there will be fearful sights and great signs from heaven (Luke 21:11).

Do you know Jesus? Do you know who He is? He is the sinless Son of the Living God. He is the living Word of God. He spoke the truth in the past. Everything He said will happen in the future. A choice is given to us. The Lord has spoken of blessings and curses. He has spoken about life and death. Now it is our time to choose. I choose blessing! I choose life! How about you? Know Him! Love Him! Obey Him! This will open the heavens for Him to pour out blessing and favor for you, your family and your church. Listen to the witness of John the baptizer:

And John bore witness, saying, "I saw the Spirit descending from heaven like a dove, and He remained upon Him. I did not know Him, but He who sent me to baptize with water said to me, 'Upon whom you see the Spirit descending, and remaining on Him, this is He who baptizes with the Holy Spirit.' And I have seen and testified that this is the Son of God" (John 1:32-34).

As the Lord kept all His promises given to John, He will keep all His promises given to you. Accept the testimony of John the baptizer! Believe in the Son of God. Love Him and obey Him and then ask Him to be your Lord and Savior! Repent and return to the Lord so that you can live under the Open Heaven now and for all eternity. Don't let another day go by without being right with God the Father through His Son, Yeshua ha Messiach!

WISDOM AND HEAVEN

We need the wisdom of the Holy Spirit to fully grasp these things. Paul says that not many of us were wise when we came to the Lord. Thank God that this lack of wisdom is not a permanent condition. Believe the promise which is released in James 1:5, "*If any of you lacks wisdom, let him ask of God, who gives to all liberally and without reproach, and it will be given to him.*" The Lord has a solution to the problem of limited wisdom. Just ask and He will provide.

People involved in higher education can help to give you more knowledge. You can study, memorize and retain lots of information. This is good! However it is only the knowledge of the things of this world. The Lord has a much higher level of revelation for you. He wants you to have both the wisdom to live well in this life but also for the wisdom of the Spirit to be given to you. When you receive the wisdom of the Holy Spirit, great understanding of the eternal realm of the Spirit will be released to you. Read aloud the passage below! Read it over and over until it takes root in your heart.

> *But the wisdom that is from above is first pure, then peaceable, gentle, willing to yield, full of mercy and good fruits, without partiality and without hypocrisy* (James 3:17).

Did you know that the word "mystery" in the Bible is supposed to mean things formerly hidden which have now been made manifest. I say supposed to mean, because there is so much false teaching on this topic. Some teach that you cannot know the mysteries of God. This is true of worldly wisdom, but it is false in terms of spiritual wisdom. The Lord wants you to know the things of the Spirit. This is a promise given to us by His Living Word. Study carefully what Jesus said to the disciples in the fourth chapter of Mark:

> *But when He was alone, those around Him with the twelve asked Him about the parable. And He said to*

them, "To you it has been given to know the mystery of the kingdom of God; but to those who are outside, all things come in parables, so that, 'Seeing they may see and not perceive, and hearing they may hear and not understand; lest they should turn, and their sins be forgiven them'" (Mark 4:10-12).

You have already turned and received the forgiveness of your sin. You are now ready to hear and understand *"the mystery of the kingdom of God."* Always keep in mind that Jesus did not just release these things to the twelve. They are for all those who believe in Him through their teaching. It is for you and it is for me. May we take hold of it and receive it by faith right now! May we see, perceive, believe and receive all the Lord wants to pour out to us from the Open Heaven. With the help of the Holy Spirit, the Spirit of truth, we can be led into all truth!

To them it was revealed that, not to themselves, but to us they were ministering the things which now have been reported to you through those who have preached the gospel to you by the Holy Spirit sent from heaven--things which angels desire to look into (1 Peter 1:12).

Peter believed that the things which were given as mystery to saints in the past were now a part of His inheritance. He encourages us to have the same faith. May the Lord release more and more of the hidden things of the kingdom to you! May you see and experience the good and perfect gifts released by the Father of lights! May you overcome every deception of the enemy and become a pillar in the temple of God! Are you a "pillar in the temple" of God? Are you an overcomer? Now is the time to believe, receive, overcome and take possession of all that the Lord has promised!

> *He who overcomes, I will make him a pillar in the temple of My God, and he shall go out no more. And I will write on him the name of My God and the name of the city of My God, the New Jerusalem, which comes down out of heaven from My God. And I will write on him My new name (Revelation 3:12).*

PRAYER

I am praying for you to live and minister under an Open Heaven. I am praying that the Lord will give you provision, protection, and powerful prophetic words through the Open Heaven over you! I pray that the Lord will release you from being bound in the natural so that you can visit Him in Heaven! I pray that the Lord will give you many experiences like the one John reported in the passage below! I release it to you in the mighty name of Yeshua ha Messiach! Amen and Amen! Read it and receive it!

> *After these things I looked, and behold, a door standing open in heaven. And the first voice which I heard was like a trumpet speaking with me, saying, "Come up here, and I will show you things which must take place after this." Immediately I was in the Spirit; and behold, a throne set in heaven, and One sat on the throne. And He who sat there was like a jasper and a sardius stone in appearance; and there was a rainbow around the throne, in appearance like an emerald. Around the throne were twenty-four thrones, and on the thrones I saw twenty-four elders sitting, clothed in white robes; and they had crowns of gold on their heads. And from the throne*

proceeded lightnings, thunderings, and voices. Seven lamps of fire were burning before the throne, which are the seven Spirits of God. Before the throne there was a sea of glass, like crystal. And in the midst of the throne, and around the throne, were four living creatures full of eyes in front and in back. The first living creature was like a lion, the second living creature like a calf, the third living creature had a face like a man, and the fourth living creature was like a flying eagle. The four living creatures, each having six wings, were full of eyes around and within. And they do not rest day or night, saying: "Holy, holy, holy, Lord God Almighty, Who was and is and is to come!" Whenever the living creatures give glory and honor and thanks to Him who sits on the throne, who lives forever and ever, the twenty-four elders fall down before Him who sits on the throne and worship Him who lives forever and ever, and cast their crowns before the throne, saying: "You are worthy, O Lord, To receive glory and honor and power; For You created all things, And by Your will they exist and were created" (Revelation 4:1-11).

PAUSE AND REFLECT

1. How did an open heaven benefit Hagar and Ishmael?

2. How did an open heaven benefit Abraham and Isaac?

3. How does faith enhance your benefits from an open heaven?

4. What came to Jesus as He lived under the open heaven?

5. How and when will your inheritance be made available to you?

6. In what ways have you experienced multiplication in your life and ministry?

7. How have you seen judgment fall from the open heaven?

8. How can you access the wisdom of God under the open heaven?

CHAPTER 13

OPEN HEAVEN A KEY TO GLORY

A s we begin to live more fully under an Open Heaven, we discover this experience itself is a key to another powerful blessing of the Lord. The Open Heaven is the key to living and ministering in the glory. We do not just suddenly start moving in the glory. It is a process. And, it often happens gradually over a long period of time. We are in essence moving from glory to glory just as the Lord leads us. Study the passage of scripture below and seek the Lord's revelation for this move of God.

> *But we all, with unveiled face, beholding as in a mirror the glory of the Lord, are being transformed into the same image from glory to glory, just as by the Spirit of the Lord* (2 Corinthians 3:18).

This passage is often used out of context, and many people miss the awesome power and freedom being released in this promise. For some it is only about angels coming to assist in their ministry. It is wonderful to see angels and have them minister with you and for you!

However, the Lord is speaking about so much more. If you want to begin to move in the glory, the important question becomes: How do we get that veil removed so that we can behold His glory? The key to this is in the three verses just prior to this one. (For a more complete revelation of this mystery, see my book, "*Seven Levels of Glory*.")

> *But their minds were blinded. For until this day the same veil remains unlifted in the reading of the Old Testament, because the veil is taken away in Christ. But even to this day, when Moses is read, a veil lies on their heart. Nevertheless when one turns to the Lord, the veil is taken away. Now the Lord is the Spirit; and where the Spirit of the Lord is, there is liberty* (2 Corinthians 3:14-17).

The most important step you can take in this lifetime is to accept Jesus Christ as your Lord and Savior. Without Him you can do nothing. Without Him you cannot experience the Open Heaven. Without Him you cannot experience the glory. Without Him you cannot be lifted from glory to glory. If you want the veil to be lifted so that you can see these things, begin again with Jesus. Then ask the Spirit of truth to guide you into all truth.

Ask the Holy Spirit to give you a deeper experience of the baptism. Ask Him to give you another baptism of fire so that you can be cleansed from everything which is hindering your movement. Remember what Paul wrote in verse 2 Corinthians 3:18, "...*just as by the Spirit of the Lord.*" All of these things are part of the work of the Holy Spirit. You cannot advance in the kingdom or in the glory unless you are led by the Holy Spirit. Only those who are led by the Spirit of God are actually the sons of God. Have you received the Spirit of adoption? Now is the time to seek it and receive it.

For as many as are led by the Spirit of God, these are sons of God. For you did not receive the spirit of bondage again to fear, but you received the Spirit of adoption by whom we cry out, "Abba, Father." The Spirit Himself bears witness with our spirit that we are children of God, and if children, then heirs— heirs of God and joint heirs with Christ, if indeed we suffer with Him, that we may also be glorified together (Romans 8:14-17).

DEEPEN YOUR UNDERSTANDING OF THE GLORY

In the New King James Version of the Bible glory is mentioned 351 times. By comparison, prayer is mentioned 108 times. Obviously glory is a very important topic, but it hasn't really had that much attention over the years. Therefore people remain confused and uninformed about the glory. Look again at what Jesus taught in the twelfth chapter of John. As you read it again, look at it through the eyes of the Spirit.

Father, glorify Your name. Then a voice came from heaven, saying, "I have both glorified it and will glorify it again." Therefore the people who stood by and heard it said that it had thundered. Others said, "An angel has spoken to Him." Jesus answered and said, "This voice did not come because of Me, but for your sake" (John 12:28-30).

Jesus did not do all these things and suffer all that pain on the cross for His own benefit. He did it for the glory of the Lord and He did it for you and for me. He wants us to be lifted higher in our understanding of the glory. He wants this so that we can step up to a higher level of His anointing. Are you ready to move up to another level of glory? Are you ready to begin to work for and with the glory of God?

> *On one occasion, while he was eating with them, he gave them this command: "Do not leave Jerusalem, but wait for the gift my Father promised, which you have heard me speak about. For John baptized with water, but in a few days you will be baptized with the Holy Spirit." So when they met together, they asked him, "Lord, are you at this time going to restore the kingdom to Israel?" He said to them: "It is not for you to know the times or dates the Father has set by his own authority. But you will receive power when the Holy Spirit comes on you; and you will be my witnesses in Jerusalem, and in all Judea and Samaria, and to the ends of the earth"* (Acts 1:4-8, NIV).

I find it interesting that Jesus had to tell them twice to wait for the power. We have seen in previous times, the disciples frequently lost their focus on the things of the kingdom. They often got distracted by other issues of their own making. Don't we do the same? Perhaps we need to hear this for ourselves. The disciples quickly went back to their own ideas about what the Lord was going to do. Over and over, Jesus had to get their focus back on the plans of God. Without the outpouring of power from the Holy Spirit, they would not be able to accomplish their mission.

> *Now when He had spoken these things, while they watched, He was taken up, and a cloud received Him out of their sight. And while they looked steadfastly toward heaven as He went up, behold, two men stood by them in white apparel, who also said, "Men of Galilee, why do you stand gazing up into heaven? This same Jesus, who was taken up from*

you into heaven, will so come in like manner as you saw Him go into heaven" (Acts 1:9-11, NIV).

Have you ever wondered what this promised return of Jesus will look like? Jesus gave us some powerful imagery about this. The angels said that Jesus would return like He left. Jesus said that there would be signs in the sun and the moon and the stars near the time of His return. We are now in the midst of a series of blood moons, a solar eclipse and showers of stars seen in the skies above us. Perhaps we need to be very alert in this hour and understand what He is saying to us. In the same way that He departed, Jesus will return on a cloud. He will also return with power and great glory! Are you ready for it? Read it again and get ready for it! Amen?

And there will be signs in the sun, in the moon, and in the stars; and on the earth distress of nations, with perplexity, the sea and the waves roaring; men's hearts failing them from fear and the expectation of those things which are coming on the earth, for the powers of the heavens will be shaken. Then they will see the Son of Man coming in a cloud with power *and* great glory*. Now when these things begin to happen, look up and lift up your heads, because your redemption draws near (Luke 21:25-29).*

HOLY SPIRIT RELEASED FROM HEAVEN

Just as Jesus promised, the Holy Spirit fell on them with power in Jerusalem on the day of Shavuot (Pentecost). Have you noticed that Jesus has kept all of His promises in the past? This should build your faith that He will keep all of His promises in the future. Believe what He promised! Then receive it by faith! It really isn't all that complicated.

The Lord has made it easy for us. Hear Him say to you, "Ask and you will receive!" Then ask for all these precious and powerful outpourings of the Holy Spirit.

If you have not been baptized in the Holy Spirit and with fire, you need to seek that right now! Perhaps you need to go to a Spirit-filled church and have the elders lay hands on you as Paul did in Corinth. Whatever it takes, you must be baptized with the Holy Spirit and with fire to move with Him in this season of the Glory. As you read and study the passage below, ask the Lord to do for you what He did for all of the believers assembled that day.

> And suddenly there came a sound from heaven, as of a rushing mighty wind, and it filled the whole house where they were sitting. Then there appeared to them divided tongues, as of fire, and one sat upon each of them. And they were all filled with the Holy Spirit and began to speak with other tongues, as the Spirit gave them utterance (Acts 2:2-4).

I really love the passage of scripture you just read. I like to read it over and over and each time ask the Lord for a greater outpouring of the Holy Spirit and for more fire. I want to be fired up for the Lord and to have all the power and glory needed to minister this gospel to the lost. I am excited about what the Lord has done, what He is doing, and what He will do in the future. And, I love to have the opportunity to tell others about it and prepare them to receive it. I love to lay hands on people and see the Holy Spirit do His work again. It is awesome and holy every time.

Think about it! Pray for it and seek it with all your heart! Time is short and the Lord will return soon. While we wait, power and glory are available to us for this time and this season. It is your time to be ministering in the glory. By this I mean that at the same time we are obedient to do our assigned work under our God-given anointing, we are expecting the glory to fall at any moment on the people. The glory I am talking about is the heavy weighty presence of the Lord. Sometimes it is so heavy that it presses you down and you cannot move. While you are covered with the glory like a heavy blanket, the Lord Himself ministers to you through the Holy Spirit. This is far better than anything we can do in the anointing.

Amazing things happen in the glory. I remain hungry for this all the time. I am always thirsty for more of His glory. When it comes, you will feel like you are drinking the new wine of the Kingdom. You will feel like you are becoming drunk in the Spirit as the wine saturates your whole being: spirit, soul, and body. It feels like the fresh oil of Heaven is being poured out to you and everyone around you as the Lord heals all your hurts, pains, sorrows and sicknesses. The power of God charges the air like a powerful field of electricity. Sometimes your skin feels like it is being covered with electrical current and that someone (the Spirit or an angel) is touching you. It is like the sweetness of honey and you begin to taste it and see that the Lord is good.

We are so blessed to be living in this season when His glory is being poured out to us from Heaven. As you begin to experience more and more of the Open Heaven, you can expect these things to manifest more often. Are you ready for it? The Lord is good and His love and mercy endure forever and ever. Wouldn't you like to feel that for yourself? All you have to do is ask, knock and seek. He is faithful to provide. I am expecting more and more of His glory to manifest as we wait for His return. I want to see what the Lord has promised for us in that season.

I will show wonders in heaven above and signs in the earth beneath: Blood and fire and vapor of smoke. The sun shall be turned into darkness, and the moon into blood, before the coming of the great and awesome day of the LORD (Acts 2:19-20).

Steven saw it when he was being stoned for his faithful service to the Lord. *"But he, being full of the Holy Spirit, gazed into heaven and saw the glory of God, and Jesus standing at the right hand of God, and said, 'Look! I see the heavens opened and the Son of Man standing at the right hand of God!'"* (Acts 7:55-56) That is really awesome. However, I want to see it now rather than just moments before my death. I believe the Lord wants to give it to me and to you. How about you? Do you believe this? Then receive it by faith right now!

As he (Paul) journeyed he came near Damascus, and suddenly a light shone around him from heaven. Then he fell to the ground, and heard a voice saying to him, "Saul, Saul, why are you persecuting Me?" And he said, "Who are You, Lord?" Then the Lord said, "I am Jesus, whom you are persecuting. It is hard for you to kick against the goads" (Acts 9:3-5).

Paul didn't experience the glory while Jesus was still in His earthly ministry. He was so stuck to his old ways of seeing and thinking that he was not open to what Jesus was releasing. He was so caught up in manmade doctrines that he didn't see that Jesus was speaking the truth of Father God. He missed the time when Yeshua was releasing a powerful anointing in the glory to all who would believe. Don't miss it in the time of your visitation!

He was fighting against what the Lord was doing. Jesus compared this to kicking against the "goads." These were sharp sticks that shepherds used to control the sheep. Kicking the end of a sharp stick doesn't do much damage to the stick, but it can cause you a great deal of pain. That is what Paul was doing. To be awakened, Paul had to be hit with so much of the glory that it left him blind for three days. This happened to slow him down enough for the Lord to teach him what he needed to know and to prepare him to receive the ministry of one of the believers coming to heal his blindness.

I pray that we will not resist the Lord this way. Yes, the Lord did a mighty work in the life and ministry of Paul. But, think about what he could have experienced if he had walked and talked with Jesus for those three years of His ministry. Think about the delight in his soul to have personally witnessed the resurrection of Jesus which he spent the rest of his life proclaiming. May we not wait and miss so much of what the Lord is doing with His awesome glory in our generation!

The glory can come to you in many different ways. You may be in a glory outpouring when it hits you with so much power and weight that you are pinned to the floor for an extended period while the Lord ministers to you. It may come as a blinding revelation from the Lord when you least expect it. It may come as a result of your hunger and thirst as you cry out for more of His presence. It may come in a vision, a dream, or a trance. However it comes, embrace it and never let it go! Peter was touched by His power and glory when he saw heaven opened in a trance.

Then he became very hungry and wanted to eat; but while they made ready, he fell into a trance and saw heaven opened and an object like a great sheet bound at the four corners, descending to him and let down to the earth (Acts 10:10-11).

239

It took a trance for Peter to see heaven opened again. The Lord has different ways for each of us to be opened to receive it. Jesus promised Nathaniel that he would see heaven open and angels ascending and descending on the Son of man. If Jesus said it, I believe that Nathaniel saw it. When Peter, James and John experienced an Open Heaven on the Mount of Transfiguration, they also witnessed the glory of God in the radiance of Jesus' appearance. They saw the cloud of the Father's glory. Then they heard the voice of the Lord coming from the cloud of His presence. They also saw Moses and Elijah. Would you like to have experiences like this? Ask and you shall receive!

The three disciples on the Mount of Transfiguration were so overwhelmed in the glory that they didn't know what to say or do. It took Peter and John several years to even be able to talk and write about it. Now it is your season to experience the Open Heaven and the Glory of the Lord coming upon you. Remember: the Open Heaven is the key to entering into the glory of the Lord. The more you experience of the Open Heaven, the more you are enabled to experience the glory.

A day is coming when the righteous in Jesus Christ will all be able to enter into the city of the Lord and experience His glory and His light forever and ever. But why wait? Begin to live in it now. Seek it with all your heart. Be part of the generation of Jacob: those who seek His face! Read the passage below and receive the promise for yourself. Don't wait! Do it now!

But I saw no temple in it, for the Lord God Almighty and the Lamb are its temple. The city had no need of the sun or of the moon to shine in it, for the glory of God illuminated it. The Lamb is its light. And the nations of those who are saved shall walk in its light, and the kings of the earth bring their glory and honor into it. Its gates shall not be shut at all by day (there shall be no night there). And they shall bring the glory and the honor of the nations into it. But there shall by no means enter it anything that defiles, or causes an abomination or a lie, but only those who are written in the Lamb's Book of Life (Revelation 21:22-27).

The promises in this passage are awesome and I am looking forward to seeing them with my own eyes. How about you? I am stirring these things up in my heart right now (2 Timothy 1:6 (NKJV), "*I remind you to stir up the gift of God which is in you through the laying on of my hands.*") I am fanning the fire of God into a flame in my own heart (2 Timothy 1:6 (NIV), "*For this reason I remind you to fan into flame the gift of God, which is in you through the laying on of my hands.*") Now is the time for you to be fanning the flame and stirring up the gifts of God which were released to you through the laying on of hands. Call out for the Holy Spirit baptism, for the fire of God, and for the manifestation of the Glory in your own life! Then call for them to manifest in the lives of your family members, your church and your ministry!

But you, beloved, building yourselves up on your most holy faith, praying in the Holy Spirit, keep your-selves in the love of God, looking for the mercy of our Lord Jesus Christ unto eternal life. And on some have compassion, making a distinction; but others save with fear, pulling them out of the fire, hating even the garment defiled by the flesh. Now to Him who is able to keep you from stumbling, and to present you faultless before the presence of His glory with exceeding joy, to God our Savior, Who alone is wise, be glory and majesty, dominion and power, both now and forever. Amen (Jude 1:20-25).

PRAYER

*Grace and peace be multiplied to you in the knowl-
edge of God and of Jesus our Lord, as His divine
power has given to us all things that pertain to life
and godliness, through the knowledge of Him who
called us by glory and virtue, by which have been
given to us exceedingly great and precious promises, that through these you may be partakers of the
divine nature, having escaped the corruption that
is in the world through lust. But also for this very
reason, giving all diligence, add to your faith virtue,
to virtue knowledge, to knowledge self-control, to
self-control perseverance, to perseverance godliness, to godliness brotherly kindness, and to brotherly kindness love. For if these things are yours and
abound, you will be neither barren nor unfruitful in
the knowledge of our Lord Jesus Christ. For he who
lacks these things is shortsighted, even to blindness, and has forgotten that he was cleansed from
his old sins. Therefore, brethren, be even more diligent to make your call and election sure, for if you
do these things you will never stumble; for so an
entrance will be supplied to you abundantly into the
everlasting kingdom of our Lord and Savior Jesus
Christ (2 Peter 1:2-12).*

PAUSE AND REFLECT

1. What are some of the benefits of Holy Spirit baptism?

2. What are some of the ways you can experience the glory?

3. What have you experienced in the glory?

4. What are you doing to position yourself under the open heaven?

5. What can you do to stir up these gifts in your spirit?

CHAPTER 14

THIRD HEAVEN VISITATION

HEAVEN OUR HOME

Many people get upset when I tell them about third heaven visitation. I am certain that there are many reasons for this. One of the primary reasons seems to be a belief that others cannot accept the things I have experienced if they have not had that experience. This belief flows right out of a spirit of pride. This is a very dangerous spirit, and we must do whatever it takes to avoid this spirit. Being under the oppression of a spirit of pride makes you vulnerable to the spirit of Leviathan (see my book, "A Warriors Guide to the Seven Spirits of God, Part 1).

The spirit of Leviathan twists everything. It will twist your understanding, your words, and your logic. It will lead you into much error. It will make it very difficult for you to understand the truth of God's Word. Remember what the Lord said to Job: "*On earth there is nothing like him (Leviathan), which is made without fear. He beholds every high thing; He is king over all the children of pride.*" (Job 41:33-34) If you have a spirit of pride, it will make Leviathan your king and you will not be able to understand the deep things of God. You need true humility to understand and experience Third Heaven visitation. Notice that Paul's humility prevented him from claiming this experience as his own.

> *I know a man in Christ who fourteen years ago—whether in the body I do not know, or whether out of the body I do not know, God knows—such a one was caught up to the third heaven. And I know such a man—whether in the body or out of the body I do not know, God knows—how he was caught up into Paradise and heard inexpressible words, which it is not lawful for a man to utter. Of such a one I will boast; yet of myself I will not boast, except in my infirmities. For though I might desire to boast, I will not be a fool; for I will speak the truth. But I refrain, lest anyone should think of me above what he sees me to be or hears from me (2 Corinthians 12:2-6).*

Paul was not the only man to have an experience like this. There are many references in the scriptures to those who were caught up into Heaven. It is clear to me that Isaiah, Ezekiel, and John all had this experience of being caught up into the third heaven. Read John's experience in the passage below and seek to experience what he experienced. See if you can feel what John must have felt as this unfolded for him.

> *After these things I looked, and behold, a door standing open in heaven. And the first voice which I heard was like a trumpet speaking with me, saying, "Come up here, and I will show you things which must take place after this." Immediately I was in the Spirit; and behold, a throne set in heaven, and One sat on the throne. And He who sat there was like a jasper and a sardius stone in appearance; and there*

was a rainbow around the throne, in appearance like an emerald. Around the throne were twenty-four thrones, and on the thrones I saw twenty-four elders sitting, clothed in white robes; and they had crowns of gold on their heads. And from the throne proceeded lightnings, thunderings, and voices. Seven lamps of fire were burning before the throne, which are the seven Spirits of God. Before the throne there was a sea of glass, like crystal. And in the midst of the throne, and around the throne, were four living creatures full of eyes in front and in back (Revelation 4:1-6).

In the same year in which the king died, Isaiah was lifted up to heaven and saw the Lord seated on His throne. He was totally shocked by what he saw. It was so powerful that Isaiah thought he might die. He couldn't understand how a human being who was caught up in the sins of the flesh could see the holy and powerful God of heaven and live. Read the passage again and try to get a feel for what Isaiah experienced. Let go of all your previous knowledge of the passage and try to experience it again as if you are Isaiah and you have been caught up into heaven! Think about what you would feel and think if this was happening to you.

In the year that King Uzziah died, I saw the Lord sitting on a throne, high and lifted up, and the train of His robe filled the temple. Above it stood seraphim; each one had six wings: with two he covered his face, with two he covered his feet, and with two he flew. And one cried to another and said: "Holy, holy, holy is the Lord of hosts; The whole earth is full of His glory!" And the posts of the door were shaken by the voice of him who cried out, and the house was filled with smoke. So I said: "Woe is me, for I am undone! Because I am a man of unclean lips, and I dwell in the midst of a people of unclean lips; for my eyes have seen the King, The Lord of hosts" (Isaiah 6:1-5).

Ezekiel had amazing experiences of the glory of God. Read the first two chapters of his book again and try to experience what he must have felt and thought during these amazing open heaven moments. Over and over the Lord did amazing things to teach Ezekiel what he needed to know in order to fulfill his calling as a prophet to Israel. These open heaven experiences eventually led to his being lifted up into the heavens with the Lord and seeing even more amazing things. As you did with Isaiah, read his experiences again and try to experience his thoughts and feelings.

In the sixth year, in the sixth month on the fifth day, while I was sitting in my house and the elders of Judah were sitting before me, the hand of the Sovereign LORD came upon me there. I looked, and I saw a figure like that of a man. From what appeared to be his waist down he was like fire, and from there up his appearance was as bright as glowing metal. He stretched out what looked like a hand and took me by the hair of my head. The Spirit lifted me up between earth and heaven and in visions of God he took me to Jerusalem, to the entrance to the north gate of the inner court, where the idol that provokes to jealousy stood. And there before me was the glory of the God of Israel, as in the vision I had seen in the plain (Ezekiel 8:1-4).

After all of his amazing experiences with the risen Lord Jesus, Paul felt a deep hunger and even a groaning in his spirit for more of the glory. He wanted to be clothed with glory. He wanted to transcend the dwelling in the flesh and experience more of heaven. He wanted to literally be swallowed up in the life of God and by the life of God. Can you identify with this deep hunger and unquenchable thirst? I want more of Him! I want more of his presence! I want more of His glory! I want to spend more time in heaven with Him. How about you? As you read about Paul's hunger, let you hunger grow until you experience the same groaning and earnest desire to be clothed with the glory of God and to be swallowed up by life!

For in this we groan, earnestly desiring to be clothed with our habitation which is from heaven, if indeed, having been clothed, we shall not be found naked. For we who are in this tent groan, being burdened, not because we want to be unclothed, but further clothed, that mortality may be swallowed up by life (2 Corinthians 5:2-4).

The day of the Lord's return is growing close. Some people grow weary waiting for it. Some have given up. But I am leaning forward in the foxhole waiting for the day of His return. A soldier leaning forward in the foxhole is ready for the battle. He is about to step out of his protective surroundings and launch a powerful attack on the enemy. He is ready to get out of a defensive posture and go on the offense to take the battle to the enemy.

Real warriors run toward the sound of battle rather than running from it. Now is your season to lean forward in the foxhole. Don't grow weary in your spirit waiting for His return. When you have done all to stand, keep standing in faith for that day. Don't quit when the time of His return is so close at hand. I like the way Paul said this to the church in Roman.

And do this, knowing the time, that now it is high time to awake out of sleep; for now our salvation is nearer than when we first believed. The night is far spent, the day is at hand. Therefore let us cast off the works of darkness, and let us put on the armor of light. Let us walk properly, as in the day, not in revelry and drunkenness, not in lewdness and lust, not in strife and envy. But put on the Lord Jesus Christ, and make no provision for the flesh, to fulfill its lusts (Romans 13:11-14).

Paul had a very clear vision of that day and felt it rapidly approaching. He longed for it. He pressed in to it. He cried out for it. He worked to help others build up their expectations for the coming of that day. He didn't want anyone to miss it. Because of this love of God in his heart, Paul had a great hunger in his loving heart to win the lost. How about you? Can you feel it? Does it give you a heart for the lost? Are you pressing in to it and calling out for others to wake up, watch, and remain alert for this great and awesome day? Get a feel for Paul's heart in the two passages below.

For the Lord Himself will descend from heaven with a shout, with the voice of an archangel, and with the trumpet of God. And the dead in Christ will rise first (1 Thessalonians 4:16).

And to you who are troubled rest with us, when the Lord Jesus shall be revealed from heaven with his mighty angels (2 Thessalonians 1:7, KJV).

SCRIPTURAL AUTHORITY FOR
THIRD HEAVEN VISITATION

I want to base all of my beliefs on the Word of God. When I began to experience Third Heaven visitation, I wanted to be certain that it was of the Lord. I wanted to be certain that it was clearly revealed in God's Word. One of the first passages which the Lord revealed to me was in the second chapter of the book of Ephesians. This passage has become the foundation of my theology on Third Heaven visitation.

And God raised us up with Christ and seated us with him in the heavenly realms in Christ Jesus, in order that in the coming ages he might show the incomparable riches of his grace, expressed in his kindness to us in Christ Jesus (Ephesians 2:6-7, NIV).

Do you really believe this? Many people who call themselves Christians do not really believe this. Some even change the passage to say what they believe. They say that this is something we will experience in the future after we die and go to heaven. However, this is not what Paul writes. He says that this has already happened. Perhaps his own third heaven visit convinced him of this. You have already been raised up with Christ and you were seated with Him in heavenly places as soon as you were born again.

God is doing this now in order to prepare us for what is to come. In the future (ages to come), He will show the exceeding riches of His grace by the kindness he has already shown us in Christ Jesus. We are now living in that age Paul was talking about in this passage. Remember: you don't get your inheritance after you die. An inheritance is something you receive now because someone else died. Jesus died so that all the riches of the Father's grace could be given to you now and for all eternity. Hallelujah! Thank you Father God! Trust me in this: you need this now as you are part of the generation raised up to live and serve in these last days!

As I continued to study this second chapter in Ephesians, I noticed that the promise is restated in verse eighteen. Along with Jesus, we are given access to the Father in Heaven by the work of the Holy Spirit. This verse built my faith up even higher. Over time, the Lord revealed more and more to me about this passage. He had been doing a work in me for several years before I experienced my first Third Heaven visit and I had not been aware of it.

One year, the Lord told me to begin to pray for Israel every day. I began to do that right away. The way I obeyed the Lord was to get face down before Him every morning and cry out for Shalom in Jerusalem. A few days later I expanded that to all of Israel. The prayers kept being refined over time and I began to pray the Aaronic Blessing (Numbers 6:24-27) over them and to call out for the sevenfold Shalom of God to be given to them. This is how I understood the sevenfold Shalom: peace, provision, protection, prosperity, productivity, power, and prophetic words to guide them to Father God through Yeshua ha Messiach. It is still my practice to pray this daily.

The year following the Lord's command to pray for Israel, He told me to begin to acknowledge and participate in all His appointed times. I had been doing a Passover Seder each year for several years. I really liked to do this because it was the time in which the Lord released us to experience His communion. But, in those earlier years, I had not done much with the other appointed times. In fact, I didn't have a very good understanding of these times. Notice that I am using the terminology, "Appointed Times." This is significant. The Hebrew word "mo-ed" was not properly translated in the earlier versions of the English Bible. It was translated as "feasts." However, the original meaning is appointed time or season.

The first appearance of this Hebrew word is in Genesis 1:14, *"And God said, "Let there be lights in the expanse of the sky to separate the day from the night, and let them serve as signs to mark seasons and days and years,"* In this verse the Hebrew word "mo-ed" was translated as "seasons." The sun, the moon and the stars were set in the Heavens to mark the seasons (appointed times) of the Lord, holy days of observance, and both the Shabbat (Shemitah) and jubilee years.

Remember God had already created light in verses 3, *"And God said, "Let there be light," and there was light."* We didn't need the lights in the sky so much to see as to know the spiritual times and seasons of the Lord. Like the sons of Issachar we need to know the times and what the Lord wants us to do. (1 Chronicles 12:32, *"of the sons of Issachar who had understanding of the times, to know what Israel ought to do,"*)

The year following my observance of the appointed times of the Lord, I began to experience Third Heaven visitation. I had not noticed the connection in the beginning, because it happened over this three year period of time. The revelation of this came slowly as I shared these things with others. Then I was given another profound piece of this promise so that I could understand more fully the meaning of this Word from the Lord. To discover it for yourself, study what follows. If you want to receive it, look again at what Paul was teaching in Ephesians. It is when Jewish believers and Gentile believers come together that this promise is fully released.

For He Himself is our peace, who has made both (Jew and Gentile) one, and has broken down the middle wall of separation, having abolished in His flesh the enmity, that is, the law of commandments contained in ordinances, so as to create in Himself one new man from the two, thus making peace, and that He might reconcile them both to God in one body through the cross, thereby putting to death the enmity. And He came and preached peace to you who were afar off and to those who were near. For through Him we both have access by one Spirit to the Father (Ephesians 2:14-18)'

Did you catch that? It is somewhat subtle until the Holy Spirit brings wisdom and revelation to enlighten us. Paul is making this strong connection between our relationship with Israel and with other believers as a key component of the promise of access to Him through the Holy Spirit. This is exactly what I had experienced during those three years. These experiences really became full as my wife, Gloria, and I began to travel to Israel every year. During those trips, we made many connections with Jewish people living in Israel.

Before these connections were made, we prayed but did not receive the fullness of the promise which came from establishing relationships in Israel. Over the years, we have prayed for many people there and have been amazed by the healing power available to them in this season. We have had the opportunity to witness about Yeshua to many Jewish people on these visits. To our great joy, we have seen several accept Yeshua as Messiach. We have made a partnership with a messianic pastor and some of his church leaders. Each new level of relationship has brought more glory and more depth to the Third Heaven visits.

The Lord has so much more for you. You can see several things which are being released as you continue to study the second chapter of Ephesians. In Yeshua, you have been given citizenship in heaven. Wow! Isn't that awesome. But the Lord gives even more. He has made you a member of His household and is building you up to be his dwelling place. Hallelujah! Study the promises in the passage below and begin to celebrate and give thanks to our awesome Father God!

Now, therefore, you are no longer strangers and foreigners, but fellow citizens with the saints and members of the household of God, having been built on the foundation of the apostles and prophets, Jesus Christ Himself being the chief cornerstone, in whom the whole building, being fitted together, grows into a holy temple in the Lord, in whom you also are being built together for a dwelling place of God in the Spirit (Ephesians 2:19-22).

Paul wrote again about our citizenship in heaven. If you are a citizen, you should have access. If you are a member of the household of God, you should be able to visit in the house. If you have an intimate and loving relationship with Jesus, you should be able to spend time with Him. If you love the Father and accept His promises, He opens the heavens for you and He may lift you up at any time. As you study the passage below, claim your citizenship in heaven more than you have ever done before.

For our citizenship is in heaven, from which we also eagerly wait for the Savior, the Lord Jesus Christ, who will transform our lowly body that it may be conformed to His glorious body, according to the working by which He is able even to subdue all things to Himself (Philippians 3:20-21).

This is your season to claim the promises of scripture and begin to move in these awesome things of the Lord. This is your season to visit in the throne room of heaven. Isaiah saw it. Ezekiel saw it. John saw it. Why not you? Claim it and ask the Holy Spirit to do this for you! Now is the time to go boldly before the Throne of Grace! Study the passage below and ask for wisdom and revelation to fully understand it. Then claim it for yourself!

For we do not have a High Priest who cannot sympathize with our weaknesses, but was in all points tempted as we are, yet without sin. Let us therefore come boldly to the throne of grace, that we may obtain mercy and find grace to help in time of need (Hebrews 4:15-16).

PRAYER

For this reason I bow my knees to the Father of our Lord Jesus Christ, from whom the whole family in heaven and earth is named, that He would grant you, according to the riches of His glory, to be strengthened with might through His Spirit in the inner man, that Christ may dwell in your hearts through faith; that you, being rooted and grounded in love, may be able to comprehend with all the saints what is the width and length and depth and height—to know the love of Christ which passes knowledge; that you may be filled with all the fullness of God. Now to Him who is able to do exceedingly abundantly above all that we ask or think, according to the power that works in us, to Him be glory in the church by Christ Jesus to all generations, forever and ever. Amen (Ephesians 3:14-21).

FOR MORE ON THIRD HEAVEN VISITATION

If you desire to learn more about the subject of Third Heaven visitation, I recommend that you study my book, "_Beyond the Ancient Door_" I was commanded by the Lord to write this book to help others find the open door to Heaven. Over a period of several weeks, the Lord lifted me up and taught me the contents of this book. In reality, it is His book! You can find it at many online book stores. You can also find it on our website at: www.highercalling-ministriesintl.com

PAUSE AND REFLECT

1. Which oppressive spirit comes against the proud? What effect does it have?

2. How did a heavenly visit impact Isaiah?

3. What did Ezekiel see, hear, and believe about heaven?

4. How did the third heaven visit effect Paul's Ministry?

5. What connection can be made between observing the Lord's Appointed Times and Third Heaven visitation?

6. Describe the connection between the one new man concept and access to heaven.

SUMMARY

Vision: Saturday, August 9, 2014

Shabbat Shalom!

L ast night, during worship, the Lord gave me a vision of a great divide between the darkness of our world and the light of His Glory. I saw a door open to Heaven. The light of His glory which was the color of amber was shining out with great intensity. In the darkness, I saw someone standing just outside the door looking intently inside. This person had a sword in his left hand. It was not raised in either a defensive or offensive way. It was pointing downward and slightly in front of the person as if trying to feel his way along in this place and to sense any danger. This person's attitude was very timid and cautious.

I wanted to cry out to the person and tell him to enter the door, but I could not communicate with him. My heart longed for this person to step forward and enter into the awesome glory of the Lord. As I prayed intently for the person to summon up the courage to move forward, I suddenly realized that this vision was speaking of something in each of us. There is a hesitancy to go into new and unknown places. There is a hesitancy to step into the fullness of His power and glory. I prayed a prayer based on 2 Timothy 1:7, "Lord you have not given us a spirit of fear. You have given us power, love and a sound mind. May we realize it and live in the power of it every day! Give us courage to approach your glory!"

In worship this morning, I was given what appeared at first to be a very different vision of an opening into His Glory. It was not up in the Heavens. It was not like a door or window on the same level where I was standing. It was an opening into the ground. I had never seen an open portal into heaven like this before. Great light and great glory was pouring out like amber fire. I saw many small animals coming close to look into the light of His glory.

At first, I was amazed by their lack of fear, but then another awesome thing came into my mind. People were moving around nearby seemingly oblivious to this portal into His Glory. The animals, on the other hand, seemed to have a greater ability to sense the glory than the people who had been made in His image. I marveled at the difference between this vision and the one I had received the night before. Then the Holy Spirit led me to remember Balaam's donkey in Numbers, Chapter Twenty Two:

Then the Angel of the Lord stood in a narrow path between the vineyards, with a wall on this side and a wall on that side. And when the donkey saw the Angel of the Lord, she pushed herself against the wall and crushed Balaam's foot against the wall; so he struck her again. Then the Angel of the Lord went further, and stood in a narrow place where there was no way to turn either to the right hand or to the left. And when the donkey saw the Angel of the Lord, she lay down under Balaam; so Balaam's anger was aroused, and he struck the donkey with his staff (Numbers 22:24-27)/

Balaam was obviously a seer, but there were things in Balaam's life which prevented him from seeing clearly in the Lord's spiritual realm. He was using occult practices to see. These demonic gifts didn't help Him when the angel of the Lord appeared. So the Lord revealed the angel to Balaam's donkey. Apparently the donkey's spiritual eyes were wide open. I believe now that Balaam's donkey actually had an advantage because he had not been influenced by the spirit of religion or by occult practices. He had no manmade doctrines to prevent him from seeing and believing what the Lord revealed to him in the spiritual realm.

I wanted to pray for the seer anointing of this donkey to come onto the entire body of Christ. (Just joking! Or am I?) I pray that you will earnestly seek to discover if there are things in your soul or your spirit which are hindering your ability to see the glory! I pray that the Lord will give you courage and strength to step into His light and to be empowered by His Glory! Amen!!! I encourage you to pray earnestly for what Paul taught in Romans, Chapter Twelve:

I beseech you therefore, brethren, by the mercies of God, that you present your bodies a living sacrifice, holy, acceptable to God, which is your reasonable service. And do not be conformed to this world, but be transformed by the renewing of your mind, that you may prove what is that good and acceptable and perfect will of God (Romans 12:1-2).

I am praying this for you and for me right now! I ask the Lord to do a mighty work in you. May He release a powerful transformation to your soul through the renewing of you mind! May you see things the way He sees them! May you do things the way He does them! May your spiritual eyes be opened wide so that you can see and do what the Holy Spirit is leading you to do in this season! Amen and Amen!

Pray with me as I continue to pray earnestly for your spiritual eyes to be opened much wider! I pray that you will be enabled to quickly see the moves of the Lord so that you can move with Him! I pray that you will never miss the presence of His Glory or an opportunity to step through the open door in Heaven! Don't resist it because it comes in an unexpected form. Remember what the Lord said in Revelation 21:5, *"Then He who sat on the throne said, 'Behold, I make all things new.' And He said to me, 'Write, for these words are true and faithful.'"* May you always remain open to the new things of Father God! Amen! As I prayed this prayer, I remembered Elisha's simple prayer for his servant:

> *So he answered, "Do not fear, for those who are with us are more than those who are with them." And Elisha prayed, and said, "Lord, I pray, open his eyes that he may see." Then the Lord opened the eyes of the young man, and he saw. And behold, the mountain was full of horses and chariots of fire all around Elisha* (2 Kings 6:16-17).

Elisha's prayer was so simple and spoke directly to the servant's need. We try to complicate things with big words. Some prayers look like an attempt to draw attention to the person rather than to the Lord. They try to impress others with their ability to speak eloquently. They sometimes pray as if this is a work of their own making. We need to thoroughly and completely get the message. It is all about Him and what He has already done for us.

This is a time to simplify our prayers and our practices. This is a time to speak directly to the needs of others. As

I thought about these things, I started to pray for you and for me again. Lord, open our eyes that we may see! Lord open our eyes to see your Glory! Lord, open our eyes to see the presence of your "horses and chariots of fire." Lord help us to increase in faith to know with certainty that *"those who are with us are more than those who are with them."* Amen!

I pray for the Lord to open your eyes to see what He is doing so that you can do it! I pray for you to see and hear what He is saying so that you can say it! Jesus said that we would be able to do what He did and even greater things. I pray that you will read this aloud over and over until it is anchored in your spirit and your soul. Today, may you focus your faith on the words of Jesus in John, Chapter Fourteen! May these things be released to you so that you can move in the fullness of the blessing and in the power of His might! May you accomplish all He has called you to do!

> *Most assuredly, I say to you, he who believes in Me, the works that I do he will do also; and greater works than these he will do, because I go to My Father. And whatever you ask in My name, that I will do, that the Father may be glorified in the Son. If you ask anything in My name, I will do it. If you love Me, keep My commandments. And I will pray the Father, and He will give you another Helper, that He may abide with you forever—the Spirit of truth, whom the world cannot receive, because it neither sees Him nor knows Him; but you know Him, for He dwells with you and will be in you* (John 14:12-17).

Lord make this real in our minds and hearts! Give us a heart to perceive, eyes to see and ears to hear all you are saying to us today! Lord give us the courage to move in the power of Your Word! Amen and Amen!!!! As I finished praying the visions ended. May this bless you as much as it blessed me!

HEAVEN AND THE FINAL JUDGMENT

Before completing this book, I felt compelled to mention one more of the times when people will experience an open Heaven. A day is coming when everyone – great and small – good and evil will experience an Open Heaven one last time. Your future in eternity depends on your readiness for this season. It is the season of the Final Judgment when everyone will stand before the throne of God. On that day everyone who is not in Christ will face their final judgment. They will be judged according to their works. That is a frightening thought.

I don't want anyone to be ignorant of this coming season of judgment. The Lord has been so good to us in the current season of grace that many people have lost sight of the time which is near. It will be a time of great awe. Many who have never known the fear of God will understand it fully on that day. Unfortunately it will be too late. That day is described in the eleventh chapter of the book of Revelation:

Then the temple of God was opened in heaven, and the ark of His covenant was seen in His temple. And there were lightnings, noises, thunderings, an earthquake, and great hail (Revelation 11:19).

On that day, every knee will bow and every tongue will confess that Yeshua is Adonai! On that day everyone will finally understand who He. They will know and understand the authority and power which has been given to Him. They will know what it meant for their future when they chose to ignore Him, rebel against Him and live in disobedience to His Word. But, this knowledge will not benefit them on that day. It will be too late to change what is written in the books.

Now I saw heaven opened, and behold, a white horse. And He who sat on him was called Faithful and True, and in righteousness He judges and makes war. His eyes were like a flame of fire, and on His head were many crowns. He had a name written that no one knew except Himself. He was clothed with a robe dipped in blood, and His name is called The Word of God. And the armies in heaven, clothed in fine linen, white and clean, followed Him on white horses. Now out of His mouth goes a sharp sword, that with it He should strike the nations. And He Himself will rule them with a rod of iron. He Himself treads the winepress of the fierceness and wrath of Almighty God. And He has on His robe and on His thigh a name written: KING OF KINGS AND LORD OF LORDS (Revelation 19:11-16).

People will not be able to plead their innocence or ignorance on that day. The Lord revealed the truth centuries ago. We have had our chance. On that day there will be no second chances. There will be no restoration or redemption. It will be over and eternity will open for everyone. Some will go into the Father's rest to be loved and blessed forever. Others will go to a place of torment where they will have an eternity to reflect on the choices they made. Don't be deceived into believing this will not happen. It has been decreed and the Lord will do it. Remember what John said about that day:

Then I saw a great white throne and Him who sat on it, from whose face the earth and the heaven fled away. And there was found no place for them (Revelation 20:11).

People who have never known or acknowledged the fear of the Lord will know it on that day. Many will want to run and hide. But, there will be nowhere to go. There will be no place to hide. I believe the last part of that verse is also a judgment. No place will be found for them in the New Jerusalem or in the New Heaven. My heart goes out to them now and I want to cry out in this season while it is not too late. You have a chance now for redemption. Please do not miss this opportunity!

Try to picture it in your mind and then seek to see it with your spirit. John warned those living in his time that they were living in the last hour (1 John 2:18). If it was the last hour then, what is it now? We have been lulled to sleep by the clever and deceiving words of the enemy released through the leaders of this age. People have stopped looking. They have stopped waiting. And the great tragedy is that when we should be most alert, so many of us have fallen into a deep spiritual sleep.

The end will come like a flood: War will continue until the end, and desolations have been decreed. He will confirm a covenant with many for one 'seven.' In the middle of the 'seven' he will put an end to sacrifice and offering. And on a wing of the temple he will set up an abomination that causes desolation, until the end that is decreed is poured out on him (Daniel 9:26b-27).

By human power you cannot stop a flood. Once the Lord releases the desolations which have been decreed, no power on earth will be able to halt them. It is up to us to listen to the prophecies given in the Word of God, and to let the Holy Spirit guide us to make the right choices. Father God sent Jesus to get us ready and teach us to stay ready. Jesus didn't change the outcome for the world but He will change our outcome if we will let Him. I want to be ready for His return! How about you? Now is the time! This is the season! Jesus gave a warning.

For days will come upon you when your enemies will build an embankment around you, surround you and close you in on every side, and level you, and your children within you, to the ground; and they will not leave in you one stone upon another, because you did not know the time of your visitation (Luke 19:43-44).

The day of our visitation is now. May we open our eyes to see, our ears to hear, and our hearts to perceive! The Lord wants to dwell with you right now! He sent Jesus to make a way. He gave us so many awesome promises. If we love Jesus and obey Him, we will be under the fullness of the love of the Father. Then He will come and dwell with us. If we have made a place for Him in our hearts now, He will have a place for us on that day. If we have learned to fear Him properly now, we have nothing to fear in the future. I want to say that again: If you develop a Biblical and holy fear of God now, you will have nothing to fear in the future. All of Heaven is ready to shout:

And I heard a loud voice from heaven saying, "Behold, the tabernacle of God is with men, and He will dwell with them, and they shall be His people. God Himself will be with them and be their God. And God will wipe away every tear from their eyes; there shall be no more death, nor sorrow, nor crying.

There shall be no more pain, for the former things have passed away." Then He who sat on the throne said, "Behold, I make all things new." And He said to me, "Write, for these words are true and faithful" (Revelation 21:3-5).

Is His tabernacle with you now? This is the source of our hope and faith in His word. By faith in Him we can discover and hold to the evidence of things hoped for. Now we have a future and a hope which will be released at His coming. Remember when He said in Luke 21:28, *"Now when these things begin to happen, look up and lift up your heads, because your redemption draws near."* The heart of the Father is for you to be able to look up now and receive your redemption.

Jesus paid a huge price so that you could receive it. I pray that we will give Him everything He bought and paid for with His precious blood. All you have to do to receive it is repent, begin to love Him, and make it your aim to be obedient. Then all these things will be released to you! You can have them now and enjoy them forever!

Pray now: Father God I am so grateful to know that you did all of this for me! I now repent of all my past failures, sins and rebellion against you. I ask for your forgiveness! I ask for Yeshua ha Messiach to be the Lord of my life! I want to love Him and obey him so much that I will receive the fullness of your love! I want you to come and dwell in me and with me now! Father, I am placing a claim on all your promises. I bend my knees right now and confess that Yeshua is Adonai. Father release your redemption upon me and begin now to restore my soul from glory to glory into the image you have for me! I pray this in the mighty name of Yeshua ha Messiach! Amen!

I believe that if you prayed that prayer and truly intend to lead a life of love and obedience to the Lord, you were born again. I believe that all these blessings have been released to you. I believe that you have been saved from the curse by the blood of Jesus. Did you receive it?

I am crying out now, "Even so, come quickly Lord Jesus!" I pray that you are ready for the dawning of that glorious day! I pray that you will one day see the fulfillment of one of the most awesome promises in the Word of God. I pray that you will not only see the New Heaven and the New Earth, but that you will reside there for eternity! Amen and Amen!

And he carried me away in the Spirit to a great and high mountain, and showed me the great city, the holy Jerusalem, descending out of heaven from God, having the glory of God. Her light was like a most precious stone, like a jasper stone, clear as crystal (Revelation 21:10-11).

PRAYER

Jesus spoke these words, lifted up His eyes to heaven, and said: "Father, the hour has come. Glorify Your Son, that Your Son also may glorify You, as You have given Him authority over all flesh, that He should give eternal life to as many as You have given Him. And this is eternal life, that they may know You, the only true God, and Jesus Christ whom You have sent. I have glorified You on the earth. I have finished the work which You have given Me to do. And now, O Father, glorify Me together with Yourself, with the glory which I had with You before the world was. I have manifested Your name to the men whom You have given Me out of the world. They were Yours, You gave them to Me, and they have kept Your word. Now they have known that all things which You have given Me are from You. For I have given to them the words which You have given Me; and they have received them, and have known surely that I came forth from You; and they have believed that You sent Me (John 17:1-8).

TRULY THIS END IS THE BEGINNING!

OTHER BOOKS BY THIS AUTHOR

"A Warrior's Guide to the Seven Spirits of God" - Part 1: Basic Training, by James A. Durham, Copyright © James A. Durham, printed by Xulon Press, August 2011.

"A Warrior's Guide to the Seven Spirits of God" - Part 2: Advanced Individual Training, by James A. Durham, Copyright © James A. Durham, printed by Xulon Press, August 2011.

"Beyond the Ancient Door" – Free to Move About the Heavens, by James A. Durham, Copyright © James A. Durham, printed by Xulon Press, April 2012.

"Restoring Foundations for Intercessor Warriors" by James A. Durham, Copyright © James A. Durham, printed by Xulon Press, May 2012.

"Gatekeepers Arise!" by James A. Durham, Copyright © James A. Durham, printed by Xulon Press, February 2013

"Seven Levels of Glory" by James A. Durham, Copyright © James A. Durham, printed by Xulon Press, June 2013

"100 Days in Heaven" by James A. Durham, Copyright © James A. Durham, printed by Xulon Press, August 2013

Available Online www.highercallingministriesintl.com